"The commanding general had until this time believed it impossible that any troops in his command could have committed so disgraceful an act as this which now blackens the fair fame of the Army of North Carolina. He finds, however, that he was sadly mistaken, and that the ranks are disgraced by men who are not soldiers, but thieves and scoundrels, dead to all sense of honor and humanity, for whom no punishment can be too severe."

- Brigadier General Innis N. Palmer, 1864

Dedicated To History Hunters Everywhere. May You All Find Your Own Scoundrels.

Front cover:

Brevet Major George Wallace Graham, 1869, Courtesy Frontier Army Museum, Fort Leavenworth, KS

NOT A SOLDIER, BUT A SCOUNDREL

The Lives and Deaths of George W. Graham

KILLED AGAIN.

The notorious Major Graham, whose obituary has been published in all the papers in this vicinity several times during the past two years, is on hand again for another announcement of the same kind. He is the best subject for newspaper items, and the poorest man to stay dead, that this western country has ever produced. Our readers remember him as a dashing young army officer who was stationed at Fort Leavenworth about five years ago, who sported a killing mustache, a gold-headed cane, a fast horse, and was generally a duck of a man, till he was court-martialed and dishonorably dismissed the service. They will remem-

By Heidi M. Crabtree

All rights reserved. This book or any portion thereof
may not be reproduced or used in any manner whatsoever
without the permission of the publisher
except for the use of brief quotations in a book review.

Copyright © 2015 by Heidi M. Crabtree

ISBN 978-0-692-55710-5

Printed in the United States of America

5th Edition, 2018

Author may be contacted at

hmcrabtree@reagan.com

Acknowledgements

- Thomas E. Buffenbarger at the US Army War College Library - Historian friends from Fort Leavenworth who always indulged my discoveries in the area, including the staff of the Fort Leavenworth Lamp, Jeff Wingo of the Public Affairs Office, Russell Ronspies at the Frontier Army Museum - Sue Cochran at the Royal Gorge Regional Museum & History Center in Canon City, CO - Rob McIlwraith at the Letter Drop Inn in Rosita, CO. Not only did they provide me with a great meal, they let me photograph the picture of James Pringle seen in this book - The Research Center of the Utah State Archives and Utah State History, especially Heidi Stringham, who searched the dark recesses for me - The Ellis County Historical Society in Kansas sent me many fabulous old articles - Lance Christensen at the Colorado State Archives - Amy O'Neal, Washington County Library, Plymouth, NC - Ryan P. Semmes, with the Congressional and Political Research Center: Ulysses S. Grant Presidential Library, Mississippi State University Libraries - The staffs of the National Archives in Washington, D.C. and the Army specialists. I appreciate not being thrown out over giggling fits in the research room after finding a report that a Navy officer complained to McClellan that his soldiers were "laughing at his boat."

Col. (Ret) Wade Sokolosky for sharing info, understanding the obsession - The History Place, Morehead City, NC - The Libraries of Craven and Carteret Counties, NC - Duke University Rubenstein Rare Book & Manuscript Library - Richard Phillips and website North Carolina Union Volunteers/southernunionists.com - Leonard Wiggins, with whom I had the most fascinating conversations with regarding Carteret family histories - Richard Phillips and his website for the NC Union Volunteers - Tom Sherlock at Colorado Health History.

Kathy Golden at the National Museum of American History - The Missouri Historical Society Archives - Patty Nicholas and the Forsyth Library, Fort Hays State University - Francis S Duffy III and his family. I felt as if I were back in time as I talked to this fascinating man, a descendent of "the spy-trader," and who even looks like his ancestor. The Fort Wallace Museum, Wallace, KS.

Everyone at the New Bern Historical Society. Claudia Houston for the initial help and history, and Mickey Miller for indulging an ersatz Josie, and bringing a less serious Georgie to life one chilly Halloween weekend.

I appreciate my husband, Lt Col James D. Crabtree, for letting me have "another man" in my life, and for taking care of the cats while Mom was away on Scoundrel Safaris. James, you need a goatee…

If I have left out anyone I truly apologize and it in no way reflects on my gratitude. It's been a long set of train tracks.

Frontier Army Museum - Fort Leavenworth KS – 2012

I wish there had been an electrifying moment to recount upon seeing Major George Wallace Graham's face for the first time in early 2012. The handsome cavalry officer was self-assured but would not look me in the eye. Scars visible on his skin hinted at a storied past. But why would he not look at me if he had a tale to tell? I went on to other faces in that photo file.

In later attempts to find stories to match those faces, some of which *were* bold enough to look back at me, I learned that Major Graham had served in North Carolina during the Civil War, the state I would eventually return to. His picture was taken in 1869 when he was already a Civil War veteran and leader of a company of troops stationed in Kansas. Maybe he looked so self-assured because he never would have believed that his career would soon be over.

Turns out, Graham was willing to tell his story after all, or at least tease me. I moved back to North Carolina, not too far from the scene of his first heroics and scandals. I became hooked on chasing this man's past.

In July 2014 I stood on a dusty road in Colorado near places with names right out of Wild West novels, like Poverty Gulch, and within view of what one of the locals told me was the old hanging tree, soon to be torn down since it was now as lifeless as the bodies it once displayed. Alone, armed with nothing more than a photocopy of a picture of an old mine, I located the scene of lost lore and quietly absorbed my surroundings. The mine wasn't a hole in a mountain with faded and loose boards keeping me from certain death. I tauntingly spoke Graham's name aloud, expecting anything and nothing. There was no sound but that of gusts warning me that a storm was coming. No strange whistling in the wind. Driving back to Fort Collins, in a strong downpour, I thought of this adventure that had fallen into my lap. I had to return home to turn boxes, books and plastic containers full of papers into The Story, with the hope that others would be as fascinated as I was.

Did he hear me? One coincidence led to another, and what at first seemed like setbacks or postponements were another twists in the plot. Years of synchronicity make me think about the objects on my shelf collected from around the country, and the Carte de Visite of Graham himself, found by a dealer in Colorado.

This may be the definitive George. Many things have been added and the style is, hopefully, more readable. I don't call myself a professional writer but be assured that I am a meticulous researcher who at least double-checks facts, and doesn't always trust primary sources. I've walked paths, coastlines, stayed in antebellum buildings, built family trees, left the National Archives with my clothes dirty from digging through files, racked up travel miles, and pestered people. Oh, and the cost of buying things like that CDV, and the 24th Rockett Battery diary, among other goodies. I asked a friend who is a psychologist if I am "obsessed." He told me something I'll never forget - "In order to do a good job on anything, you have to be obsessed."

For whatever reason, I'm in the world of light, representing this man in darkness, for better or for worse…

Life as a Hardened Young Man

His first life began in Crown Point, New York on October 16, 1839. Or 1840. Or was it 1842, as he would sometimes claim? Up in Essex County, NY mild summers were, as now, followed by beautiful, orange-red autumns leading to snowy winters. Farms dotted fields. Businesses sprang up, especially in the lumber industry. The proximity to water drew young men to work. There was no shortage, for example, of men who worked on the boats that frequented Lake Champlain, or those who drove canal boats using horses. So trafficked was the area that a new lighthouse was built a few years before war broke out, and "boatman" was used to describe a variety of jobs.

He was the second son of George and Harriet Gould Graham, who were married by a Justice of the Peace in Bridport, Vermont in 1830. By the time George, the youngest, was born, he had two older brothers, William and Charles, and three older sisters, Nancy, Martha, and Sarah. The oldest was also a girl, Mary Ann, who died in 1852 from unknown causes.

George was listed as Wallace Graham in the federal and state censuses for New York. Nothing has been found before 1855 for the family, and that census shows he was living with an uncle, Charles Gould, along with his brothers, and Sarah. Place of birth was listed as Vermont, and this would change from Vermont to New York occasionally. George Jr. probably went by Wallace, or his mother called him Wallace anyway, to avoid confusion with papa George. Later letters from Harriet will lend credence to this.

Young George grew up close to historical sites that were already old by the time he roamed the area. Did he wander around Fort Ticonderoga, or think about the military past at old Fort St. Frederic? What did he read about those places? Nothing is known about his education and we can only look at his Civil War writing to guess. He was more literate and a better writer than many of his peers at that time. George also seemed to be a quick learner.

In 1860 he was just another boatman on the lake with his brothers, employed by and living at, Nathan Ingalls's hotel, on the site of an early tavern.

Why were the children not living with their parents? Their father simply disappears; indeed his birth information remains a mystery. Later census records on the children, now adults, list their father as having been born in Scotland. George Sr. either died before 1855 or walked away from his family and never returned. He is not buried in Forest Dale cemetery where much of the family lies. Harriet was living with an older man as a sort of housekeeper or attendant and sent the children to live with her brother. The family must have been quite poor.

George shows up after the war[1] with occupation listed as "Army." He was living with his brothers, Electa, and Harriet. Addendum mentions Graham's claim that he was a

---

[1] New York State Census, 1865

sergeant upon initial enlistment and now (1865) a captain. Graham would frequently fudge his past, sometimes for reasons we can guess at, and others lost forever.

So Graham had no father figure other than perhaps Uncle Charles. Maybe he grew up resentful, especially if his father had walked away, leaving them in the care of someone else. He was probably a bright boy, but had a very mischievous side. Living without his mother, and his siblings married with their own worries, he may have been lonely, and running at night, getting mixed up in trouble.

As a teenager, Graham, living with the Ingalls as a boatman, was used to horses. We also know he could be a handful because years later Harriet would hint at her son's transgressions in a letter from a typical mother worried about her son. So it may have been no surprise when he was arrested in 1857. Teenaged George had been sent to New York's Clinton (Dannemora) Prison for committing 3rd degree burglary in Washington County in January of that year[2], and he later bragged about as much to fellow Army officers, some of whom wrongly guessed that he'd attempted to kill someone, or that he was only paroled if he would enlist in the Army, both incorrect. Who knows what other youthful indiscretions had Harriet worried?

Dannemora literally had a dungeon in those days. It was not uncommon for a prisoner to be hung upside down as punishment for any infraction. He was sentenced by Judge Enoch Rosekrans, who had a reputation for being droll, and would speak his mind and be a smart aleck to the accused, eliciting laughter from those present. Graham, along with others involved in that burglary, John May, Michael Bruin, and Gilbert Traver, would not be free again for some time. Prison records show that he was 5'8" tall, with light brown hair, grey eyes, and a light complexion. And scars. George already had scars on his knee and chest. He was released early in 1860. On a cold winter's day, he faced his future in Crown Point, NY and returned to the same work.

By the time rumbles of secession and war began, he was only 20 or 21 years old with a prison term behind him. He may have been angry about his father, hardened by whatever cruelties may have been done to him in that prison, and now back to a dead end life as a boatman on Lake Champlain. His recollections of living with his mother and having someone to show care for him were already just childhood memories. We shall see by his later treatment of women that he was given a bad example by a father who likely walked out on them.

When the war broke out his brother William enlisted as a private in the 34th NY Infantry and quickly transferred to the 5th U.S. Cavalry in 1861. Seeing William enlist may have given Graham ideas. Perhaps he simply wanted to leave a stifling Crown Point life. He might have had a desire to do the right thing. Did he want to explore the country and make a hero of himself, or show up his brother, who was probably getting attention after he returned home from an injury? Was it possible he was taken in by the "futuristic" nature of a certain unit? Whatever the reasons, when he enlisted on Oct 15, 1861 as a 2nd Lieutenant in the 24th New York Rockett (original spelling) Battery,[3] events that would change many lives were set into motion.

---

[2] New York, Clinton Prison Admission Ledgers, 1851-1866, 1926-1939

[3] NARA RG 94. Entry 501 Records and Pension Document File #320519 and Entry 496 VS File #1693-VS-1876. To prevent confusion the unit Graham served in will be referred to as the 24th NY Battery, which is how it

According to military documents, in October 1861, he signed on for a term of three years, mustered on Dec 7, and was commissioned two days later. In those early days of the war men were often made lieutenants by votes from other soldiers. Given what we will later see about Graham, he may have bought drinks to encourage the others into voting for him, or he may have bragged about some experience that he did not have. With his born ego he probably envisioned some of what was in his future. That ego would not have imagined how it would end.

From the same town was Congressman John Hammond, who would become a Union general and prominent citizen, as well as president of the Crown Point Iron Co. Hammond certainly knew of the Ingalls hotel and likely saw the Graham boys plodding along the water. It would be the last time George would drag a canal boat around.

---

would be known throughout much of the war.

Life as a Civil War Officer

2nd Lt. Graham and the 24th New York Battery traveled to Washington D.C. in anticipation of joining Gen. Ambrose E. Burnside's move into coastal North Carolina. The waterways of the Pamlico and Albemarle, as well as the river Neuse, were strategically important to the Union, which needed a staging area for seaborne attacks on the Confederacy. Confederates held the town of New Bern, sitting on the Neuse, but fell to Federal forces, causing the rebels to retreat inland to Kinston.

Much had been made of those early rockets used in the 24th, those terror weapons that would herald a new way of warfare. At the outbreak of the Civil War a Londoner, Thomas Lion, made his way to New York to both push the Congreve Rocket and get financial backing to make an improved Congreve a miracle weapon for the Union. Lion, competing with others who wanted government contracts, wrote to Secretary of War Simon Cameron in the same month that Graham enlisted. Lion offered his service to any rocket units that might be organized. He may have been shocked when his proposition was approved the same month. The rocket idea had one big plus: men with little training could use it, enabling more battalions to quickly be raised.

Cameron gave the authorization for one Rocket Battalion, with Lion in charge. Fate had intervened on Graham's future when the plans were given to Gen. Barry of New York, in command of the Artillery of the Army of the Potomac, while New York would muster the troops. Gen. Barry would call for any man, skilled or not, for this exciting new battalion to be nicknamed Barry's Battalion in his honor. Graham was one of these young men, perhaps tempted by stories about the fantastic weapon.

Thankfully for us, a correspondent calling himself "Drummer" was writing to the Wyoming (NY) Times and thrilling readers with news about the unit. Graham was apparently one of the first fifty men to sign on. In Buffalo another twenty or so joined before recruiting went on to Albany. In that city, The Ladies of Albany welcomed the soldiers with a large meal of turkey, chicken, and oysters.[4]

When Graham was in Albany he met Lion, who was now a Major. Graham would get used to publicity, as the big magazines of the day picked up the story of these not so secret, amazing weapons. The Nov 23,1861 issue of Scientific American boasted in an article about the formidable weapon that would be used to protect the coast, reading in part, "It is said to be one of the most fearfully destructive weapons ever devised by man." The piece also claimed that it was likely going to be paired with a "more remarkable invention, whose name we withhold till it shall be required by the government," a combination predicted to be able to "utterly annihilate" any hostile forces.

Two companies were thus formed, with Graham a 2nd Lieutenant in Company B, under command of Capt. Jay Lee. George would soon be on his way to Washington via New York City where the men spent a few days at Park Barracks due to being delayed by a heavy fog. Most men took advantage of the unexpected break by sightseeing. The

---

[4] Original diary of an unnamed 24th Rockett Battalion soldier. Author collection

barracks themselves were not attractive to the men, who found most of the city an "Elysium of Loaferdom."[5]

The 24th traveled through Philadelphia and Baltimore. In Philly, The Ladies of Philadelphia gave the men another big meal. In return, the men gave cheers and "a Tiger for the union." Capt. Lee himself wrote that the people of both cities "greeted us as warmly and entertained us as generously, as though we were the first soldiers who had passed through their cities, and as though we were the sole saviors of the country."[6] Graham no doubt surveyed the cheering crowds and liked the applause.

Finally arriving in Washington, the rocket men set up at Camp Congreve near the Capitol building after a night or two in temporary barracks, which the men nicknamed Tongue Barracks because all they were fed was coffee, bread, and tongue. Here they also slept on bare floors in terribly cold weather.[7]

Concerning the new rockets, the Wyoming *Times* had at least one other correspondent from the troops, nicknamed "Quartermaster," who wrote long reports and reviews of those weapons. They varied in size, according to letters, as being 12-20" long and 2-3" wide. Other than the cone shaped iron tip, the rockets were hollow, to hold a "secret inflammable compound." Its fuse was on the tail of the rocket. They were said to be extremely noisy and the rockets used in training, though old, did yield some good results. The men pointed the rockets on their stands at a 45° angle across the Potomac, and the rockets flew a good three miles. A plan was made to hollow out the iron heads as well and fill them with balls and powder. The soldiers were told that four rocket tubes would be carried on each caisson, like any artillery battery, and the men's weapon would be a "terror to treason."

Graham and the rest of the battery remained in Washington for months. It wasn't until March that they received their guns and carriages, with horses arrived a week later. During that time while the men waited for weapons and equipment nothing much was done besides the usual drilling and training with sabers. Naturally a few soldiers managed to find trouble. Petty jealousies made them accuse officers of favoritism. Men grew sick over the winter and several died from illness.

An unnamed correspondent for the Wyoming *Times* mentioned a wild ride with Graham. Graham was the type who couldn't sit still for long. He had an itch to explore, along with a growing desire to push the rules to their limits. Writing from Camp Congreve in December 1861, the correspondent tells about their quarters, a tent with a stove in the middle with a dirt floor. On Christmas Day this person left camp with Graham; one or both wanted to see the "land of secesh." Graham and comrade took a few horses and rode down Pennsylvania Ave. despite being stopped several times by sentinels telling them to slow down. They made it as far as Falls Church, Virginia before turning back, finding the town unimpressive and in need of repair.

Despite early successes, it didn't take long for the members of the 24th to call their formidable weapon "the fizzle." On the 1st of April the men received their first rockets, with more coming mid-month, but by May they were complaining that the "improved"

---

[5] Merrill, *Records of the 24th Independent Battery*, 1870
[6] Ibid.
[7] Original diary of an unnamed 24th Rockett Battalion soldier. Author collection

Congreves would, once fired, go in any direction, sometimes curving and hitting the men themselves. The soldiers debated whether Lion actually knew what he was doing. They were all growing tired of waiting for the improvements on equipment and launchers, and feared they would miss leaving for North Carolina. Target practice was still held with an old blanket as the target until an unknown person, tired of these misfired missiles, stole the blanket.

On April 28, 1862, they boarded five schooners headed for North Carolina. In Alexandria, the 3rd NY Cavalry joined them. The weather would give the boat captains hell for many weeks as they tried to get the soldiers safely to North Carolina. On the last day of April as they were entering Chesapeake Bay, a tug came from Washington to stop them from going any further. Anchored somewhere near the area where the Potomac meets the bay, a few bored men took a rowboat to Charon Island and brought back a large amount of oysters.[8] Perhaps George was one of the adventurous men who were too wound up to stay on board the boat, where most of the guys complained that they had no room to even stand in the areas where they slept.

Early in May, an unknown soldier writing in his diary tells us that they passed the York River in the dark, early morning hours of the 3rd, and that he could see flashes and hear heavy guns. Later that morning they reached Fortress Monroe, where countless vessels were lying offshore. The USS *Monitor* was visible to the men, and they were anchored just in line of the "Rip Raps," renamed Fort Wool at about this time. The captain had taken their schooner out from Fortress Monroe, but the wind was blowing the opposite direction. Back they went to Monroe and anchored again. Taking a small boat, a few men left the schooner for the fortress itself and brought back a copy of the previous day's New York *Herald*. This was the first real news any of the men had heard since leaving Washington.

The wind would not change until May 6th, and a cold rain off and on would add to the boredom. The only thing breaking up the monotony was another trip by a few men to shore for a *Herald*, gun noise from Norfolk, and the CSS *Virginia* (*Merrimac*) coming within sight of Monroe with a large lot of ladies conspicuously aboard, preventing the Union from firing upon her. The men noted such things as Craney Island and boats whose names they knew, the Naugatuck for example. Later that day they did leave, with Cape Hatteras as the next goal, and passed Cape Henry. Later that day, President Lincoln arrived at Fortress Monroe with Secretary of War Stanton and others aboard the USS *Miami*. George had just missed seeing the President. The *Miami*, by the way, would play a role in the lives of many of these men in Plymouth, North Carolina less than two years later.

They reached Hatteras the next day and anchored about five miles offshore due to winds threatening to push them onto a sand bar. On May 9th they set on for their final destination: Newberne. The trip through Albemarle Sound and up the river would be tricky as it was easy to run aground or get stuck on rocks. When the men first saw Newberne, they noticed the large amount of pines as well as "masked batteries" left behind by the Confederates. Countless vessels lie offshore as the US flag flew. The soldiers were able to see a bit of the city from the boat, noting churches, heavily shaded streets, and what they first thought was a majority of buildings made of brick. Walking the town later, a diary

---

[8] Original diary of an unnamed 24th Rockett Battalion soldier. Location of this "Charon Island" unknown. Author collection

author noted that most were actually made of wood, and found it curious that the homes here had chimneys on the outside, instead of totally contained within. They compared the streets and sidewalks to their own up north, noting that these were all dirt. Once on shore, everyone stated hearing the inevitable rumors, ie, that Richmond had fallen. One of their guards was shot just four miles outside of town. They also noted the terrible state of Newberne, having had large areas burnt by retreating Confederates, and how there seemed to be more blacks in the city than whites. Indeed many whites had fled to cities such as Kinston. One family that remained was that of John Fisher Jones, who owned the Washington Hotel, on the site of the current fire station. Jones's hotel was one of the buildings burned, and instead of leaving town the family took up in a house at the corner of Middle and Broad streets.[9] The smiles on the newly free blacks' faces were also apparent. Any large, undamaged quarters were taken over by Union troops and officers. The 24th were just outside the city. Soldiers wandered into woods as far as they dared where they both loved the wild berries and hated the flies and mosquitos. A few also discovered British made minie balls embedded in trees. An unidentified soldier wrote in his diary that in March, when the first of Burnside's troops arrived, Confederates flew a US flag over a nearby bridge to fool Union gun boats, then set fire to that bridge as they left town.

May was a very rainy month. The 24th drilled and stood guard in the rain, dealt with weather that would be cold one day and very hot the next. Men would awake soaked from rain, as they had no beds to sleep on. Snakes were a threat, and most soldiers slept with one eye open, as they were aware of the proximity of the enemy and their desire to retake Newberne. Also, diarrhea and "bowel complaints" hit just about everyone. Later in May that problem was so prevalent that sometimes no drill could be had. Rumors flew near the end of the month that North Carolina had surrendered but the men were now suspicious of any rumor. During this time a grand review of Artillery was held by Gen Foster, the rain continued, and the boys of the 24th were still waiting to move to better quarters. They were temporarily sleeping in abandoned Confederate quarters but they were apparently so filthy that sickness continued because of that.

Not much is known of Graham's early days with the 24th in Newberne, but an entry in a diary is worth a thought: "Our Officers are a set of mean Shit Asses. All they care for is themselves they cant even drill us without making a mistake…(*sic*)"[10]

At the very end of the month Burnside reviewed the troops who walked through the town. Soldiers noted that whenever Burnside passed a US flag he would remove his hat and bow his head. A wild rumor also flew through the city that Richmond had fallen and the Union had taken 60,000 prisoners!

Graham and the others found Lion preferred to be drunk much of the time, the number of troops had dwindled, and no discipline in sight.

A story went around and was taken as legit this time by the troops. Richmond had fallen and Beauregard was now a prisoner, and many men started talking about what they would do when they returned home now that it "was almost over."

---

[9] Now the location of The Chelsea Restaurant
[10] Original diary of an unnamed 24th Rockett Battalion soldier. Author collection

A letter of complaint about Lion and the whole situation with the 24th was sent to Gen. Jesse Reno, their division commander. So few men remained that companies A and B were combined, causing tension. Dissension grew until one morning at roll call when Reno was called in to set them straight. The members of B were ordered to now answer roll as members of A, or else face the guard shack. Every member answered not just with his name, not with either A or B, but with "Guard House!" Reno also let the soldiers know that Lion had been dismissed, and the same would happen to any of them if they didn't shape up. Many officers said that they would walk away and go back to the Rip Raps if split up from their original company.[11] The two companies did however wind up in different divisions. Lee's battery, Battery B, of which Graham was a lieutenant, was put in the 3rd Division. They would be sent to Newport Barracks, NC.

Listed in Volume 1 of <u>New York in the War of the Rebellion 1861-1865</u> for the date of July 27, 1862 is a report of the Battle of White Oak River involving "Graham's Battery B, Rocket Battalion" and three companies of the 3rd NY Cav. at Young's Crossroads as the men were returning to New Bern. From Heckman's report, these units, along with the 9th NJ Infantry under Major Zabriskie, left Newport (then called Shepardsville) the day prior and built bridges. They made it to Davis Mill, some 26 miles away, where they bivouacked. The next morning they arrived at Young's Crossroads with no idea that any Confederates were in the area. According to the Confederate account of the battle, which they called the Battle of Smith's Mill, these Yankees had been taking hogs from locals for food, as well as plodding through farms for vegetables. It was also reported in a Raleigh newspaper that the Yankees ransacked Pollocksville.

Col. Charles A. Heckman, 9th NJ Volunteer Regiment, sent two companies of cavalry to set up communications with New Bern. The third company was sent towards Onslow where they were surprised by a group of Confederates along the White Oak River, the Jones/Onslow county line, under Capt. Edward D. Ward. The men had crossed the river and came under fire. As the Union men fired back, including Graham with his cannon firing grapeshot, the Confederates retreated across a wooden bridge, burning it behind them. According to Union reports three rebel cavalrymen were brought back as prisoners, but the Rebel accounts list no casualties and four Union deaths. Heckman himself was wounded. Nearly three miles from the crossroads he noticed smoke coming from the rear of his column, and riding to the rear he found a large house burning, possibly the home of a Confederate colonel. He asked the soldiers if they knew anything but nothing was learned. What is interesting is that artillery was usually in the rear of the column, and that Graham later had a reputation for, among other things, burning anything he could. However, Heckman had that personality issue as well. Whatever the cause of the fire, Heckman noted both Graham and Capt. Sterns, in charge of the cavalry troops, for their assistance in his official report.[12]

The 24th had already seen insubordination, the surprising but not unexpected loss of Lion due to his drunkenness, and of course the public failure of their revolutionary weapon. Back in Washington the rockets proved to be mainly useless. Despite Newport Barracks and its lack of equipment on the part of the battery, the men were growing tighter. They were also complaining about lack of any type of training, other than drilling.

---

[11] ibid

[12] The War of the Rebellion, a Compilation of the Official Records of the Union and Confederate Armies. Series I, Volume IX, Chapter XX, page 347.

They had not engaged the enemy and had started to enjoy better billeting and meals, which they likely did not complain about.

More men were recruited for the 24th from New York, especially Perry and Buffalo. Arriving at Newport Barracks, the latest recruits found themselves labeled "the New Boys" and were treated badly by the men who had been part of the 24th since the previous winter. In October of 1862 the whole unit was re-designated as the 24th Independent Battery of Light Artillery, New York State Volunteers.[13] The great rocket experiment was finished by that summer, which was just as well since they hadn't had a connection to rockets at all since the previous spring.[14]

In early November the 24th was finally sent out on a scouting mission. Accompanied by the 3rd NY Cavalry, the 9th NJ Cavalry, and some regiments from Massachusetts, the affair was uneventful? Aside from flipping over a caisson on a tree stump and collecting some prisoners and "contrabands" (blacks), the only wounds received were bee stings after attempts to raid hives for honey.

An abandoned sawmill was discovered later in the month near the camp. Around 15,000 feet of lumber was cut and used to build winter barracks in New Bern. J.W. Merrill, writing to his family, told that the officers were all friendly and temperate, with no hostilities toward each other. He continued to say that their tents were cozy with heat from stoves. Some men built small fireplaces in their tents. The Thanksgiving meal details survive in one of these letters. The dinner consisted of two soups, boiled beef, fried pork, and stewed chicken, several vegetables, desserts, and extras such as coffee, tea, bread, and butter.[15]

On Dec 10 they left Newport Barracks for New Bern, their home away from home since summer. Gen. John Foster was about to go towards Goldsboro to destroy the important railroads. In the line, unattached to any brigade, were both companies of the 24th. Graham and the others took a route through Kinston in order to guard a crossroads. Some of the men were said to have "went to extremes"[16] in looting homes in Kinston, a sign of things to come…

On the 12th Graham, along with the 3rd NY Cavalry encountered a small group of Confederates but the cavalrymen managed to run them off. Graham later wrote in his own hand that he had been in the Battle of White Hall. Taking place in mid-December this was the raid that damaged the CSS Neuse, one of the infamous ironclads.

What happened to him next initiated his reputation as a fearless fighter, when he found himself in a large battle at Goldsboro Bridge. The Wilmington and Weldon Railroad was an important line to the port of Wilmington, NC. On December 17 Gen. Foster sent out an expedition to destroy the bridge at Goldsboro and cut that supply route. By this time Graham had managed to make himself useful in a dual role, as a volunteer aide to Heckman. It is unknown how Graham came to be an aide to Heckman, who was in a different state's regiment.[17]

---

[13] Officially changed 1863
[14] Thomas Lowry, *Civil War Rockets*, (CreateSpace Independent Publishing Platform 2012).
[15] Merrill, *Records of the 24th Independent Battery*, 1870
[16] Ibid.
[17] The answer may lie in missing letters from NARA. I attempted twice to examine letters concerning Graham

On Dec 27, Foster wrote up his report that would become the official story. He stated that Col. Heckman advanced along the track, trying to get to the bridge that was being held by Confederates. It took him two hours to reach it and, according to Foster, Graham rushed up under heavy fire to burn the bridge. It is also mentioned in this report that Graham was now an aide-de-camp to Heckman. Lt. Barnabus Mann of the 17th MA had rushed to the bridge with Graham but was pushed back when he was wounded. Foster singled out Graham in his report for the latter's conduct, writing that Mann accompanied Graham up to the bridge and Graham escaped capture by jumping off, and that he had shown much courage throughout the entire battle. He would later recount that Graham was under fire by "hundreds of muskets." Yet another account mentions Graham and Pvt. William Lemon of the 9th NJ as the two who successfully made it to the bridge.[18]

It is notable that several regiments present report that one of their men was on that bridge and assisted in the firing of it, but they all do mention Graham as well.

In any case, it is the name George W. Graham that is in the Official Records as the bridge-burning hero of Goldsborough Bridge.

Graham's name is on a state marker at Goldsboro Bridge, although erroneously listed as a member of the 23rd instead of the 24th. This is an example of the actual Official Records being incorrect. Somehow, either from those records, or some other 1862 documents, Graham is listed as having been with the 23rd and the mistake has carried on for over 150 years. It has been difficult to get the mistaken marker corrected, as primary sources are rarely questioned, so the mistake will remain until someone with the Civil War Trails association fixes it.

His name is on a list in files at NARA of officers injured during the War. He claimed to have been wounded at Goldsboro but the block where the *type* of wound should be stated was left blank, though it was probably a leg wound.

In 1911 the 17th Mass wrote their history[19]. Contained in the pages is a detailed account of the Goldsboro battle and the burning of the bridge. Graham is mentioned thus: "Graham...went forward with combustibles to fire the bridge, but returned pell-mell, and jumping behind a log, exclaimed, 'Damn them: they won't give a fellow a ghost of a chance out there.'" Col. Henry Splaine, the writer, also made note that it was "well-known" that the bridge was burned by men of the 17th Mass, specifically Willard Edmands and Lewis Besse of Company A. However, Splaine was not a fan of Graham in the first place.

A curious article ran in the Jan 5, 1863 edition of the *Spirit of the Ages*, a pro-Confederate, North Carolina newspaper. It gives the name of the Yankee who fired the bridge as "J. Duncan Graham," naming him as a Virginia native, the son of a Virginia father and Yankee mother. Could a journalist have confused Vermont with Virginia? What is even stranger is the other revelation by the *Spirit of the Ages*: members of Confederate General Beverley Robertson's staff personally knew Graham. How would Robertson's

---

at this time period in the 24th NY Ind, but those letters were not in the box I had pulled. They did a search while I waited and were obviously concerned that the papers are missing, though they were there as late as the 1980s.

[18] Drake, James M, *The History of the Ninth New Jersey Veteran Vols: A History of its Service.*

[19] Kirwin, *Memorial History of the Seventeenth Regiment, Massachusetts Volunteer Infantry (Old and New Organizations) in the Civil War 1861-1865.*

staff be acquainted with a Union officer? There was at least one possibility, to be discussed later. The only other claim in the article concerning Graham was that he was strutting about New Bern like the "Hero of the War." That would not be surprising. The tall young officer was indeed developing a swagger!

Heckman and Graham returned to New Bern earlier than the others, and Heckman later wrote in the Official Records that he intended to meet and greet the troops with a much-deserved hot meal. He and Graham were surprised to see them returning to New Bern earlier than expected. The 9th NJ had made a bet with the 17th Mass that the former would return to the city first.

On the same day as the *Spirit* article, a notice was run in the New Bern *Daily Progress* by Graham himself, seeking the return of a mare and a colt, stolen from the unit's stables on Queen Street. The idea of horses being stolen from Graham would prove ironic.

Near the end of February 1863 Graham was on a leave of absence due to a wound received while on sentry duty. He was allowed to return to New York for two weeks' recuperation. Before leaving he took it upon himself to obtain a letter of introduction from Foster to Governor Seymour of New York. The letter tells of Graham at Goldsboro Bridge and praises him as a promising young officer.[20]

The promising officer was late in reporting back for duty and reprimanded, although no specifics of his injuries and punishment have been located. What is known is that Graham was moved to Company E of the 3rd NY Cavalry by orders of Gen. Foster in late Dec of 1862 or January 1863, and was still a 2nd Lt.[21] His assignment would be temporary, and Graham's next life with yet another regiment would begin shortly. He was quickly making important friends and showing himself to be a daring cavalry officer. No doubt an endorsement form Heckman helped with his biggest assignment yet.

---

[20] George W. Graham's Personal File, National Archives, Washington DC. RG 93.
[21] The ledgers and daily books for the 24th NYIB and 3rd CAV during Graham's time are at NARA, but the pages from the time that he was a member are actually gone from the book.

Life as a Union Daredevil & Damn Yankee

General Burnside authorized the North Carolina Union Volunteers in the spring of 1862 while Graham was arriving in North Carolina. Their name also appears in other forms such as the 1st NC Regiment, 1st NC Vols, and so on. The 1st NCUV was formed at New Bern with companies A-L mustered over the next year. The NCUV was notable because, although the officers were from the North, the soldiers were enlisted from the very area where they would be engaged in fighting. They were southern Unionists, unwilling to fight for what many thought was a rich man's war, as most of them were poor farmers without big plantations or slaves. Some of these men chose to fight for the North for the $300 bounty. Others had actually been in the Confederate Army and had deserted. They were simply doing what was best at the time to feed their families, risking scorn and the label "traitor."

Possibly due to the influence of Graham's sick leave visit to New York and the Governor, as well as his connections to Heckman and Foster, he was given command of a troop of these southern Union infantrymen, with the difference being that Company L would be mounted.

On June 10th Company L was officially mustered in at Plymouth, NC. Graham must have been pushing to getting his own cavalry troop, for muster rolls located from June of 1863 lists the company as "1st Lieut Graham's Cav Co. 1st Reg't N.C. Vols" with the notation "This organization subsequently became Cav Co. L, 1st Reg't N.C. Infantry." But those rolls had been changed back Company L minus the bit about "Graham's Cavalry." He may have had his own personalized muster sheets printed, and most likely was told to stop, as he had no authority to change the name of his company.

As the reader can imagine, his soldiers were by no means popular with the locals. They would stoop to almost anything, and went along with their fearless and bullying commander, who led them into the places near their own homes for lawlessness. They definitely earned a reputation. A fellow officer from the 3rd NY Cavalry would recount later, under much different circumstances, that Graham was brave, gallant, and that he knew of many "hair-breadth escapes and daring acts."

Graham was no longer a lieutenant at a cannon or on a colonel's staff. He was in charge, near "No Man's Land," where, as he saw it, the countryside was just waiting to be plundered. Local men were away from home in the CSA leaving their farms and homes to the wives or servants. Graham's company was often somewhere in a different location than the rest of the NCUV. They spent early summer in New Bern, relocating to "Little Washington," NC in July.

Photos of members of Company L show a variety of faces from the past. One can only wonder what stories they took to their graves. Most of these men were from the area, so adding to the fact that they had to face their neighbors after the war makes those lost tales more tragic. A boy named Henderson, looking at us from across the decades, appears to be so young that one wonders how a uniform was found to fit him. His face shows the look of a determined but unsure boy. In another photo Pvt. Byrd stands next to a table, watch fob chain dangling. He also looks at the camera. At first glance he appears blank and neutral, but in his eyes is that fear mixed with determination resulting when a person does something unpopular but "right," for he proudly displays his hat on a table by his left hand. The hat is not a kepi but instead a cavalry hat with crossed sabers attached. In other posed photos of Company L that have soldiers' hats displayed, none are kepis. Graham's ego would have none of that. He now ran his own cavalry company and he would outfit his troops to stand out. Photographs of Co. L veterans taken in their old age show tales of bravery in their eyes. No matter the reader's view of the Civil War, these men probably spent their post-war lives being harassed and mistrusted. Some would take on aliases during the war and spend their lives under that name. However, it must be said in honesty, some of these Buffaloes earned the name that sticks to this day: Damn Yankees.

Damn Yanks, yes, we've heard it. But Buffaloes? That bizarre name was around before the war and subsequently attached to Unionists. Its origin is still debatable.

Perhaps the earliest reference to Unionists as Buffaloes was in Oct 1862. In Hedrick's book[22] about Unionists in North Carolina, the 1st NCUV was described as appearing so large in their uniforms that they were reminiscent of buffaloes in a herd. That same year North Carolina newspapers began writing of despicable Buffaloes in a way which tells us that locals knew the difference between "regulars" and Yankees, naming some "Union men" as Buffaloes. Yet much earlier there had been a slang term, "buffle," which meant a fool, and later someone who takes a false oath for payment. Since the pro-southerners thought of southern Union soldiers as lowlifes and traitors, serving just for the money, this could very well be the origin. Other definitions of Buffalo in this sense describe a person who cannot be trusted, or a thief. North Carolinians also related tales of "rebs spreading lies" that Northerners had one great horn sticking out of their foreheads and would eat prisoners! Educated citizens were amazed at how many people believed as much. Many Union officers in North Carolina were from New York and New Jersey so "buffalo" could have also been a reference to the large New York town by that name.[23] Whatever the origin, Hedrick wrote that in the 1st NCUV, these Buffaloes were proud of their new moniker. Graham was not yet with the NCUV when the term was used but was no doubt familiar with it. He would have to love it...fate would put that Buffalo up against his own name much later in his life.

His Co. L would have many names too. They would be known under various descriptions including Mounted Infantry, NC Union Cavalry, and Mounted Troops. Indeed, by October they did earn the pay and privileges of a cavalry unit.

Records are sketchy from that summer as far as the NCUV goes but Graham later claimed to have been involved in a fight at Gum Swamp. Gen. Innis Palmer found a sizeable number of rebels encamped in that area, which was important because of its proximity to a rail line. One of Burnside's objectives was still to cut any rail lines leading into Virginia. There were actually two battles in that area, in April and May. His cavalry company is known to have been at the second battle in May.

---

[22] John Hedrick, *Letters from a North Carolina Unionist*, (North Carolina Dept. of Cultural Resources 2001).
[23] Buffalo was also employed in a negative sense against another type of Unionist. In the late 1830s the Democrat Party split into factions, one being the anti-Tammany Hall Loco-Focos. This group fought amongst itself, some Loco-Focos wanting a union with Tammany Hall. These Unionists were derogatorily named "Buffaloes."

Graham spent the 4th of July 1863 en route from New Bern to various areas of the state. His new Co. L, along with the 3rd NY Cavalry and some artillery pieces, left town on the 3rd. The men spent Jul 3–7 not only capturing prisoners, horses, and taking around 500 contrabands, but cutting part of the Wilmington and Weldon railroad. Commanded by Lt.Col. George Lewis, Graham and these troops went to a Confederate arms factory in Kenansville, to tear up part of that rail line. Gen. Foster, senior commander in New Bern took notice of it.

Foster wanted to destroy important Confederate sites in Rocky Mount and Tarboro, and so on the 17th Co. L was ordered out again, along with the same troops from Lewis's raid but under command of Gen. Edward Potter. This operation became known as Potter's Raid.

Rocky Mount was on Foster's hit list because of its W&W railroad bridge, and important because of its location and the town's cotton mills. As for Tarboro, another Confederate ironclad was being built, along with the storehouses along the river, all of which were targets. Potter would assign the six cavalry companies and the whole cavalry regiment of the 3rd NY into individual battalions. Maj. Fenis Jacobs was assigned six companies of the 3rd, while Major George Cole commanded the other six. Graham's Company and the remaining troops were under Major Floyd Clarkson. Joining the raiders were two artillery sections, with infantry soldiers storming their way to Vanceboro on July 17 ahead of the cavalry. [24]

Early in the morning of July 18 the cavalry troops began crossing the Neuse River on their way to join those infantrymen, via way of Fort Anderson. That night the group slept near Vanceboro.

"Black Jack," North Carolina was the setting for a small attack on rebel pickets and Graham must have taken a liking to the area, as he would return the following year with more in mind.

The Union troops minus the infantrymen left for Greenville on the morning of July 19. After capturing some Confederates at Four Corners, Potter and his men easily took Greenville, as reports tell of empty entrenchments and hospitalized rebels. Blacks who had been in the local jail for attempting to join the Union in New Bern were freed, the courthouse was taken over, and looting was the order of the day. It wasn't enough to destroy the Confederate Quartermaster and Commissary stores, but residents told of private citizens being robbed of thousands of dollars, and watches and jewelry ripped right off of men and women on the street. Even before reaching Greenville an official named George Greene, who was distributing money to needy families, was robbed not only of those funds but his horse and belongings.

After the looting slowed down, Potter's men decided to hit the saloons and were drunk by the time they left that afternoon. Potter's Raiders went to Sparta by way of the Tar River Road. Gov. Vance would receive an eyewitness letter from a terrorized woman, recounting the Yankees stealing horses from citizens, breaking into homes, tying up women, taking everything from jewelry to guns and liquor. Graham and his fellows took advantage of these families, vulnerable because the men were fighting elsewhere. They

---

[24] Vanceboro was known as Swift Creek Village at this time.

all slept overnight at Sparta, probably hung-over, certainly exhausted. After a few hours of rest, the 3rd NY Cav. went on to Rocky Mount and went wild, doing the same types of plundering that they had done in Greenville. Besides destroying Confederate supplies, part of their job, they ran amok against citizens, collecting liquor, busting into homes and turning them upside down, and grabbing rings off of women's hands. A sergeant from the 12th NY Cav. commented on those actions, recalling that some Union soldiers would "go into a farmer's premises and just take what they want and destroy the rest." Whether the farmer was a rebel or a dirt-poor Union sympathizer was unimportant, and this often caused people "on the fence" to side with the Confederates.[25]

It seems that a pause is necessary here to try to explain why Graham's men robbed their own neighbors. One cannot look into the minds of each person, nor can we judge the actions of people living in a far different time. We simply do not know their reasons. Graham could have bullied these men with threats that if they did not cooperate they could be turned over to the Confederates, knowing their probably fate. Maybe some of the men did not consider Pitt County natives, for example, to be neighbors since this company recruited from along the Banks. Many were very young and possibly under the spell of Graham. He could not have been entirely heartless. Even considering his sociopathic traits, later recollections would mention that the man could be generous at times. While he may have threatened people, or ran off to the comforts of a hot meal while his men ate in fields, there were those who admired him and saw something we cannot. One private in particular would always remember his Captain.

Potter, upon arriving with the Union cavalry in Sparta, ordered a rest. While Jacobs's men went to Rocky Mount, Clarkson's were busy concerning themselves with Tarboro. Witnesses in Tarboro described the Union horsemen as having sabers, and most armed with Colt revolvers. Pushing Confederate pickets back they captured an officer and an NCO. Majors Clarkson and Cole quickly moved through Tarboro. Clarkson sent a few officers and soldiers to burn a couple of steamboats, Graham probably being one of the officers. They also burned the beginnings of a Confederate ironclad ram - Graham, never missing an opportunity to burn something may well have been one of the arsonists.

Along with torching things, the Graham's Cavalry also enjoyed looted shops and homes, and stole what they could from the Tarboro Bank. After robbing the poor cashier of his watch, they rode to his home and ransacked it. Townspeople complained to Gen. Potter, but he would simply ask for a description of the soldier, all the while knowing that too many soldiers were running loose to get a good look. He had no interest in punishing any of them. Victims felt they would be killed if they attempted to stop any looters in their homes. The local Masonic temple was even pillaged. One plundered home belonged to former NC governor, Henry T. Clark, who went out for a morning ride on his horse when he spotted the Union cavalry approaching, and the latter gave chase. Clark escaped into the woods but the raiders tore through his home, scaring his family into hiding elsewhere.[26]

While Tarboro was being vandalized some other New York troops under Maj. Clarkson were racing toward an ambush at Daniel's Schoolhouse where a few were killed and 18 taken prisoner by Confederates. Indeed, the schoolhouse became a makeshift

---

[25] David A. Norris, *Potter's Raid*, (Dram Tree Books 2008).
[26] Masonic items looted from Tarboro would later show up in the later 19th century in New York and Arizona, and returned.

hospital for wounded Union soldiers, while the Confederate side suffered almost no losses. Maj. Cole found himself and members of the 3rd NY Cav. in a similar situation while trying to assist Clarkson. Cole and troops wound up fighting part of the 17th North Carolina. The Union troops made their way with much difficulty back towards Sparta, hearing about an unguarded ford, where they made their way across in deep water with horses. By the next day, July 21, word of the incidents had spread, and so by nightfall Potter's men had contrabands following them as they were nearing the Scuffleton Bridge. The contrabands wanted to join the Unionists. These people, seeking freedom from slavery, came under attack by the Confederates that night at a plantation called Burney's Place. In trying to get back to New Bern Potter had his soldiers toss some of their looted winnings onto the roads, correctly assuming the Confederates would slow down long enough to pick it up themselves. Later, when the owners of the items tried to get them back, the rebels then turned on their neighbors, claiming that since they had run off the looters, they should get to keep what was tossed away.

Potter and his raiders arrived back at Vanceboro on July 22. Although they and their horses were exhausted they stopped for a mere four hours before riding again to Street's Ferry, opposite New Bern, before being attacked by the 17th NC Cavalry after more Confederates showed up after dark. It looked grim for the Union Cavalrymen until two gunboats and a couple of steamboats arrived. The Confederates pulled back out, west to Kinston, ending Potter's Raid.

The men were reportedly pleased with themselves, having slept so few hours, and on so little food for themselves and their horses. The southern bridges burnt had indeed had a catastrophic effect on the Confederacy. That future ironclad in Tarboro was never finished, cotton mills were gone, and warehouses full of necessary materials destroyed. Confederate prisoners captured on the raid were sent north, and the officers captured were sent to the horrible prison camp on Lake Erie in Ohio. Newspapers went wild, decrying not only Yankee scoundrels, but also the fact that they were now safe in New Bern. As for Graham, he would sit long enough to refresh and take a few breaths, and probably strut around town.

Later in the month Graham may have been as far north as Weldon. A skirmish occurred near Mt. Tabor Church and Hill's Bridge, on the Potecasi Creek. Foster ordered his men to a Confederate junction near Weldon. The rebels under Maj. S. Wheeler were pushed back, with 17 captured. Union troops at Hill's Bridge were "showing off their trophies." Capt. Splaine of the 17th Mass was said to have captured the Confederate battle flag (likely from the 12th NC Cavalry) and that the flag was sent by one of the other captains to his family as a souvenir. Splaine also commented that Lt. Graham was sporting a Colt revolver taken from a prisoner.[27]

Later, Company L, along with companies from the 12th NY Cavalry under Lt.Col. George Lewis, hit Greenville via Sparta.[28]

The summer would end as dry and hot, with locals complaining that August was even hotter than usual.

---

[27] Kirwin, *Memorial History of the Seventeenth Regiment, Massachusetts Volunteer Infantry (Old and New Organizations) in the Civil War 1861-1865*.
[28] Personal letters in the State of NY – Third New York Cavalry.

As summer wound down, Graham, always hailed as a near-perfect specimen of athleticism, took more than his share of sick leave. As is usual in researching this man, information is missing. Where others have reasons listed in their records for illnesses, Graham has none. Later that same month he was off duty again, only it wasn't from sickness: Graham was under house arrest for leaving his post too many times.

Two charges with a total of seven specifications were proffered against Graham, for violating the 42nd Article of War.[29] Graham had "habitually" abandoned and neglected his company by leaving them and his post and disappearing over several days between July 30 and August 3. The court-martial began on August 5. Col. Abram Zabriskie, 9th NY Infantry, was president, with Gen. Innis Palmer in command.

Graham's lieutenant, Thomas Fogerty, testified that Graham claimed to have been sick one of those nights the latter went missing. Fogerty stated that Graham showed him his tongue and that it "was black", and Graham said he wanted to find a doctor, but was gone all night. Fogerty claimed that Graham always left him in command when he was "unfit" for duty. It appears that this happened quite often for a healthy specimen of athleticism.

The incidents happened, to Fogerty's best recollection, near their camp at Brier's Creek. Since Brier's Creek was also said in another Civil War era publication to be located off of the Trent River, it may have been Brice's Creek. Then Fogerty was asked the location of a doctor. "In town. Between four or five miles," he answered.

The files also give us a location when the stables were mentioned. Nehemiah Ambrose, the First Sergeant, testified that his was at the junction of Craven and Broad, and Graham's at "a Mrs. Smith on _____ Street." The name of the street of this Mrs. Smith is left blank in the testimony.

Something notable is apparent in these papers; the lieutenants and NCOs always claimed that they had no idea who was in charge in Graham's absence, who kept the morning books, when their commanding officer would return from his leaves, how often he was gone, and so on. But they all were certain he was sick during those nights, apparently feeling fine and never seeking medicine during the day.

Also called to testify was John H. Curry, clerk at the Gaston House. Curry told the court information that they must have found concerning. Graham spent the nights of the 31st of July through August 3rd at the Gaston Hotel in New Bern. Curry stated under oath that Graham was first in Room 27, then moved to Room 38, and that Graham had his meals, dinner and breakfast, while there (apparently his illness and mouth issues did not prevent him from enjoying home cooking). Curry stated that Graham told him ahead of time that he would be leaving the following Monday.

Curry went on to say that he knew Graham was in his room at least some of the nights because; early on one of the following mornings, he was working outside the Gaston and saw Graham getting dressed through the window to his room. Graham himself then asked Curry a question, "Do you remember that *(illegible)* morning of the 3rd you asked me how I liked my room, what reply I made?" Curry said he may have made

---

[29] Records of the Office of the Judge Advocate General (Army), RG 153, Court-Martial Case Files, Graham, George W., MM-788. NARA.

such an inquiry but didn't really recall, but that, "Defendant said he did not sleep in his room that night." Graham never seemed to require any assistance due to an illness, according to Curry. He also basically admitted that yes, he was at a hotel.

Graham asked another question of Curry, "Do you remember me asking you if I could get a mustard plaster in the house?" "Yes," he answered, "distinctly."

A few more of his troops were called, most knowing (or claiming as much) very little about the goings-on of Company L. However, when an enlisted man was questioned whether Graham took his meals in camp, he replied that Graham claimed to have been too sick to eat. Or was he simply too stuffed from home cooking at the Gaston?

Assistant Surgeon Frederick Douglas also testified that he had noticed Graham lying upon a sofa in the Gaston House, complaining of some pain in the abdomen from handling a (*illegible*) the day before.[30] The doctor also said he met Graham by accident, and that Graham had asked for a Dr. Palmer.

After Graham signed a statement that an important witness from the 3rd NY Cavalry, Capt. Gustavus Jocknick, was unable to appear but could swear on oath that Graham had permission from Lt Col. George Lewis (also of the 3rd NY Cavalry) to remain absent, the court adjourned until August 12th when Jocknick did testify. The transcripts say that he offered absolutely nothing though as far as evidence. Graham gave a closing statement claiming that, despite Jocknick's useless testimony, Lewis did give him a verbal permission to be away from his command. Why Lewis was not questioned is anyone's guess.

He was first found "Not Guilty" on any charge, but, after "mature deliberation," he was found "Guilty" on five of the seven and sentenced to a loss of one month's pay and a reprimand in the form of a general order. Gen. Palmer added to the final report on the court-martial that he could not understand how the board arrived at their original decisions, adding:

> -- "Lieut. Graham is reminded that one of the first duties of an officer is to attend to the wants of the men of his command. This duty cannot be well performed if the officer abandons his camp for the more comfortable but less soldierly attractions of a good bed and the company of the jolly idlers around a public house." –

Later we shall consider Palmer's thoughts on an incident to come the following spring that displayed Graham's habit of running off alone, a shameful incident that hangs in the air of a small North Carolina town to this day.

A few months after this court-martial Graham went horse collecting again. According to the Southern Claims Commission[31] Graham was traveling with his company from Plymouth to Washington, NC, when they stopped at the farm of a Mr. Harmon

---

[30] Enlarging the document and comparing the handwriting to other samples has yielded no solution to what it was that Graham claimed to have lifted when he hurt himself. It almost appears that it was a few markings or abbreviations that the recorder planned to come back to sometime later.

[31] The Southern Claims Commission allowed Union sympathizers who had lived in the South during the Civil War to apply for reimbursements for losses due to Union Army confiscations.

Harrison. Harrison, 53 at the time, later testified under oath that he had nothing to do with the Confederacy and had sided with the United States, and he certainly was not in the Confederate Army.[32] Around the 1st of October, Graham and his men rode to Harrison's home and went straight for his stable, taking his only horse, a dark bay mare. When Harrison protested,

Graham himself told him, "I must have her." Harrison went to Washington, NC to get back the mare, and saw a soldier riding her around the Company L stables. Harrison spotted Graham and told him he wanted his horse back. Graham told the farmer that he would see to it that Harrison be given another horse as a replacement, but Harrison never saw any replacement or his own horse again. Records show that in 1873 the SCC gave him $100 reimbursement. A few of the witnesses for Harrison were Graham's former troops who were from the Plymouth area. In a quirk of fate, one of the men with Graham when they took Harrison's horse was a private, Horton Waters, who on Oct 1, 1883, exactly twenty years after the incident…died after an injury from a horse.

On October 18, 1863 Graham was promoted to captain. October was becoming a big month in his life, having enlisted in October of 1861, becoming a captain in 1863, and another October would prove fateful. This particular October is preserved in his oath, in his personal files, giving his promotion as a result of a vacancy and signed on Nov 24th at "Little" Washington, NC.

Graham's troops went on reconnaissance on Oct 30 along the Greenville Road and found themselves in a fight at Ford's Mill. One officer was killed, 1st Lt. James Nichol. Nichol, a sturdy, wild haired man with long sideburns, had previously been with the 3rd NY Cavalry and was just promoted to be one of Graham's officers. Maj. General Peck commanded General Order 34 be published, praising Graham and writing that Nichol "died as a soldier would choose to die." In retrospect, those orders describing Graham as "dashing" and "gallant" seem remarkable. Graham had just been promoted and on his first outing with that unit as a cavalry company he had an officer killed. Throughout the years, Graham would be described with these words again and again. Dashing isn't exactly the most important trait when being a leader, and with the exception of the Battles of Goldsboro and Wise's Forks, Graham seemed to find himself in smaller skirmishes, which he seemed to prefer. Being a scout suited him just fine. One wonders if he didn't disappear for days and return to Little Washington and explain that he was "out scouting" when he was actually looting or looking for areas to return to later. For reasons lost to history, Graham and his company were ordered by McChesney to report to headquarters.

Spending the first few weeks of November on sick call and an unspecified leave, Graham was back to duty on the 12th and back in form at Greenville.

Another General Order, G.O. 39, from Benjamin B. Foster AAG to Maj. Gen. Peck, writes of Graham's "striking and successful achievement." Interesting to note, in this letter Foster writes, "Captain R.R. West, 12th NY Cavalry, generously waived his rank to Captain Graham's familiarity with the country to be traversed." This would later be referred to in some sources as "Graham's Expedition." By the end of November we see that Graham is an expert in the area and its terrain. He, or someone, was also making sure that newspapers from New Bern to New York were hearing reports of his heroics while neglecting to mention other regiments involved,[33] and Graham was never bothered by

---

[32] Many likely sympathizers would later state that they had been loyal to the USA. Harrison did provide

monikers such as "cavalry hero of the Department" and such, as eyewitnesses would later comment on how he would strut around New Bern and Little Washington as the hero of the war. An article published a short time later changed the story slightly. West had been sent off to another area while Graham handled Greenville. West may have told Graham to take one area if he was familiar with it, while he and his own men went out elsewhere, not exactly "waiving rank" to anyone. After reading through Col. Splaine's memoirs as well what few contemporary accounts exist, it is highly possible that Graham bullied Capt. West to get command of this expedition that he attached his name to.

Graham spent on average one day per month doing Officer of the Day duties and in December took a leave of absence to New Bern on the 22nd, returning on Christmas Day.

An unexpected fight at the end of 1863 resulted in the death of another of his lieutenants, William Adams. Col. McChesney and the 1st NCUV, along with men from the 12th NY Cav and 23rd NY Arty were on reconnaissance six miles from Greenville on New Year's Eve. Confederate Major Moore tried to stop McChesney and the men from reaching Washington. There was much fighting, hand-to-hand combat, and by nightfall the Confederates retreated. McChesney ordered Red Banks Church burned. Adams was killed and a few other soldiers and horses wounded, while the Union troops were able to gain a caisson and horses from Starr's Light Battery. McChesney reported that the rebels lost a lieutenant and five men, there were perhaps more but darkness prevented an accurate count. The New Bern *Times* wrote that Graham suffered a saber cut to one of his hands.[34]

According to a newspaper blurb Graham took ten men of his company out a few days after Adams's death. They left Little Washington on an expedition with ten soldiers from Co. D of the 12th NY Cavalry to Tranter's Creek, where several men were sent back because of difficulty crossing. The remaining fifteen who did cross soon ran into a few Confederate companies. After capturing a few men from these companies, Graham approached the Confederates' main picket post where he took the uniform off of one of the captured rebels, put it on himself, and boldly walked into the camp with one of his own lieutenants, pretending he was a Confederate who had captured a Union officer. Graham's lieutenant kicked open a door while Graham allegedly thrust his uninjured hand through a window, pulled a pistol, and ordered them to surrender. Who these Confederates were is unknown, but the newspaper severely romanticized the event. Written by "A Chaplain," the story compares Graham to Ethan Allan and Napoleon, and the whole of the group as Spartans.[35] This growing reputation of Graham and the stories of the man as a dashing hero would come in handy in the future when Graham had to defend himself to the public in the American frontier. He would always put on a sophisticated face for the right people.

He and his men were all ordered to report to the Subdistrict Headquarters in the early morning hours of Jan 12, 1864 with carbines and pistols. Three days later they were at HQ again, this time fully armed and fitted out.

---

witnesses.

[34] Jan 9, 1864.
[35] New Bern Times, Jan 16, 1864

Too much gallivanting had taken its toll and he was finally ill for legitimate reasons. Diagnosed with a mild case of pneumonia early in 1864, he was on leave in Crown Point where he obtained a doctor's written diagnosis. Company books list him as leaving post on the 20th of January. Graham included a notarized statement naming Dr. J. J. Dyer as a practicing physician in Essex County. The note[36] also recommended that Graham be on leave for twenty days, putting a tentative return to North Carolina at the end of February. Why he was sent on a long trip to upstate New York to recover from pneumonia is one of those Graham mysteries. He may have wangled a way to attend to something back home, and a medical file card in the National Archives states that he returned late from leave. His excuse was apparently noted elsewhere but now lost. As is typical of Graham's files, other patient cards in that file box at NARA have a diagnosis except for Graham's. The pneumonia mention was only on the affidavit of Dr. Dyer in Crown Point.

In February Graham's company was adding horses to its stables without its leader, as company books report Lt. Fogerty, temporarily in charge of Company L, returned from parts unknown with captured horses. As far as is known, no soldiers from the NCUV were involved in the fight at Newport Barracks early in February, but some would wind up dead because of Confederate Gen. George E. Pickett's frustration at losing that attempt to retake Newport and New Bern. At least one man was added to Company L, a private by the name of Patrick Norris. Norris was an example of men who switched sides out of need for the money and responsibility to his family. Formerly a member of the 31st NC, he was captured and wound up in Union territory, enlisting in the NCUV early in 1863. He had been with Company A, pulling duty at one of the blockhouses when Graham selected him for Company L. Both USA and CSA documents exist on Norris. The physical descriptions do not match; indeed the Union description is the opposite of the way Norris was described in the CSA rolls. The NCUV may have changed his appearance knowing he was technically a deserter from the CSA in order to shield him from any Confederates that may come around looking. The NCUV did protect its men. For whatever reason, Graham gave him a more exciting job than walking the blockhouse.

Support for the Union in New Bern was strong, as evidenced by later that spring when the US flag was raised, and the town decided to light up for the evening. Homes, businesses and churches had rows of lit candles in the windows, with some offices trying to compete with others for the most illumination. Lambert & Hall, a shop, hung a sign reading "Grant, Sherman, Union, Victory, Peace." Col. Joseph McChesney of the 1st NCUV decorated his home, as did most others. The night also included a brass band concert. In about ten weeks the opinion of many Southerners in the area probably changed…and McChesney would be in New Bern as a witness in an investigation.

At the beginning of March, a fire was set outside of Little Washington, NC at an area known as Rodman's Point and at an area that saw action the previous summer. Rebel pickets supposedly started the fire by lighting bales of cotton and turpentine, and the blaze could be seen from some distance. It was assumed that Confederates set the fire, but it would be a foreshadowing of spring in that waterfront town.

Making up for lost time after his illness Graham selected troops to hit Black Jack Church again Mar 26, this time burning it. It was alleged that Confederate partisans used

---

[36] George W. Graham's Military File, National Archives, Washington DC. RG 93.

the church. Another G.O. was ordered, praising Graham and commenting how quickly and secretly the 1st NCUV was able to overcome the enemy. One officer and eight soldiers were lost and prisoners were taken. Maj. General Peck, calling attention to Graham's "dash so characteristic of a true cavalry soldier", stated General Order No 49.

A newspaper account[37] was written up in such a way as to make one wonder if the writer, under the pseudonym of *Idlewild*,[38] wasn't forming a fan club. The term Buffs was brandied about in a proud manner in lines such as, "I have to record another brilliant affair made by the irrepressible Graham and his gallant band of Buffs," and the article makes it seem as if Graham singlehandedly took on the entire of the CSA, with his second, Lt. Fogerty, showing up too late, as Graham had fought and shot his way into the rebel reserve before anyone with him knew what had happened. Eventually the enemy did draw up in a line of battle, at which time Graham withdrew, the article claiming that he gave loud cheers for both the Sub-District of the Pamlico and the flag on the way back to Little Washington.

One curious bit exists in the company books. They state that on Mar 20, Graham and another corporal left for a furlough, with the corporal returning in April. Was it merely an oversight that it was left unmarked regarding their commander coming back from leave, or were some of these exploits unauthorized? Graham certainly took liberty in more ways than one.

Graham and his superiors took license with the word "reconnaissance." No one can question the need for skirmishes and scouting. It was war. But our hero seems to have had an area of his own to use for his plundering pleasure: From New Bern and Washington in the east to areas such as Greenville and Kinston, with smaller communities in between, Graham would launch many such reconnaissance missions, returning not always with prisoners and information on the enemy, but with personal effects, liquor, horses etc. Especially horses. Graham had sticky fingers when it came to horses, and this weakness would later be his undoing, as far as the Army was concerned.

On March 25th, Graham and his men were near Black Jack Church, and came upon a few Confederates, who fled. Graham and company gave chase, finding themselves on top of a Confederate cavalry under a lieutenant named Carlton McKenzie. Undaunted, Graham and the men fought anyway, and in a mere five minutes, eight Confederates were dead, including McKenzie. A Confederate affidavit to his widow states that McKenzie died from one gunshot wound. Whether Graham fired or one of his men is unknown.

Also in March, Graham was ordered by Major Charles Graves to drill his company one hour per day. Drill was most likely at or near their stables in Little Washington. If the locals were tired of Graham and his merry men riding around town, they hadn't seen anything yet.

But most North Carolina Unionists, especially those serving with the NCUV, were demoralized after the Kinston hangings.

---

[37] New Bern Times, Apr 2, 1864
[38] Idelwild's true identity is unknown. The only clue is that his columns also ran in an unnamed New York paper.

Confederate General George Pickett, not the best of tacticians, arrived in the rather rowdy town of Kinston, NC. Kinston was typical of many of the poorer coastal areas that did not necessarily support what some locals believed was a wealthy, slave-owning class who bought themselves out of the war. There was no question as to why some of these locals went to the Union side, which gave them decent food and protection, while those on the Confederate side were dragged into a fight many of them did not believe in. This was where most men of the 1st and 2nd NCUV came in. To staunch Confederates however they were dirty traitors.

During Pickett's failed campaign, Company F of the 2nd NCUV found itself surrounded by Confederates on Batchelder's Creek and was captured and thus prisoners of a coldhearted man: Pickett. Known as the Kinston Twenty-Two, that number of Co. F men was hanged, probably near the courthouse. Eyewitness reports range from shock to those of the "they deserved it" type. Those shocked and angered included General Robert E. Lee himself.[39]

Part of the demoralization also stemmed from the CSS *Albemarle* (aka the Roanoke Ram), which aided in the Confederate re-capture of Plymouth.

Lieutenant Commander Charles Flusser was killed on April 19, 1864 in a battle at Plymouth, NC, in an engagement with his USS *Miami* and the *Albemarle*. A Navy officer who was popular with his comrades, Flusser's death was a freak accident. He fired a shell at the ram, striking its iron shell, but the shell bounced back into Flusser's vessel, killing him.

Union troops were ordered to prepare to evacuate "Little" Washington, NC. What took place on the last weekend of April 1864 would make politicians in Washington, DC take notice and leave an impression on that area to this day.

---

[39] Pickett fled to Canada after the war and even after his return to the US was still snubbed by Lee.

The Shame Of Little Washington

General Edward Harland, commanding the Sub-District of Pamlico and in charge of Little Washington was ordered to evacuate Union troops to New Bern while keeping it quiet, so citizens and even troops would not know until orders came. His instructions stated that the town not be destroyed. The 1st NCUV was to have been first on board one of the steamers, but it appears in later documents that at least Graham and his troops defied orders and stayed, taking the roads back to New Bern later. We know Graham himself did stay and had a large role in later events including the town's destruction.

It took three days to evacuate and those orders to leave didn't stay quiet for long. Someone let the secret out. The first big mistake was in not drawing up decisive plans and timelines for the units to leave town and, despite an order by Harland that any soldiers caught making trouble should be fired upon, the 17th Mass, doing Provost duty, was away from its posts and looting the 1st NCUV's quartermaster store while the streets were crawling with soldiers and a few sailors breaking into locked shops, stealing and destroying property, and dropping what they did not want on the streets. The 5th RI Arty had more than a few drunken soldiers carousing in the streets that would openly carry bottles of looted liquor on board when embarking. Shop owners recounted soldiers coming in and stealing everything from clocks and jewelry to demanding boxes of cigars and bottles of liquor. The Odd Fellows and Masonic halls were broken into and ritual items carried off. Someone started a fire at the cavalry stables that quickly spread due to wind coming off the waterfront. Homes and churches were burned to the ground, some blown up on purpose to prevent the fires from spreading. After the Union had completely left, the main part of Washington from the waterfront up to about 5th Street, and between the bridge and Respess Street, was in ruin. Townspeople state that Col. McChesney and/or his people cut off the water pumps and hoses so that the fires couldn't be extinguished, and the smoke alerted nearby Confederates that the Union troops were about to leave.

Palmer was angered and disgusted. His General Orders #5 read as follows --

GENERAL ORDERS,

HDQRS. DISTRICT OF NORTH CAROLINA, Number 5.

New Bern, N. C., May 3, 1864.

While the troops of this command may exult and take just pride in their many victories over the enemy, yet a portion of them have within a few days been guilty of an outrage against humanity, which brings the blush of shame to the cheek of every true man and soldier. It is well known that during the late evacuation of Washington, N. C., that town was fired, and nearly, if not entirely, consumed, thus wantonly rendering homeless hundreds of poor women and children, many of them the families of soldiers in our own army, and destroying the last vestige of the once happy homes of those men who have now given up all to serve their country in her of peril. And this was done by men in the military service of the United States. It is also well known that the army vandals did not even respect the charitable institutions, but bursting open the doors of the Masonic and Odd Fellows' lodges, pillaged them both, and hawked about the streets the regalia and jewels. And this, too, by United States troops. It is well known, too, that both public and private stores were entered and plundered, and that devastation and destruction ruled the hour. The commanding general had until this time believed it impossible that any troops in his command could have committed so disgraceful an act as this which now blackens the fair fame of the Army of North Carolina. He finds, however, that he was sadly mistaken, and that the ranks are disgraced by men who are not soldiers, but thieves and scoundrels, dead to all sense of honor and humanity, for whom no punishment can be too severe. The commanding general is well aware what troops were in the town of Washington when the flames first appeared. He knows what troops last left that place; he knows that in the ranks of only two of the regiments in the District of North Carolina the culprits now stand. To save the reputation of the command it is hoped that the guilty parties may be ferreted out by the officers who were in Washington at the time of these occurrences. This order will be read at the head of every regiment and detachment in this command at dress parade on the day succeeding its receipt, and at the head of the Seventeenth Massachusetts Volunteers and the Fifteenth Connecticut Volunteers at dress parade every day for ten consecutive days, or until the guilty parties are found.

By command of Brigadier General I. N. Palmer:

J. A. JUDSON,

Assistant Adjutant-General --

For whatever reason, six days later these orders were not read anymore to both the 17th Mass and 15th Conn. Also it seems Palmer had to defend his decision to send out that circular. Later articles in newspapers imply that Palmer may have received grief from Washington DC regarding that G.O. Did it bring national attention to "Yankee barbarism" adding to recent Union losses in North Carolina? What if this shameful act was partly a result of the demoralization claimed earlier? All of this would have been wonderful propaganda for the Confederacy.

The formal investigation commenced May 12, 1864 at the office of Capt. Wheeler on Middle Street in New Bern. The Board of Investigations included Col. Savage (12th NY Cav), Major Amory (2nd MA Arty), Capt. C. Smith (132nd NY Vols), and 1st Lt. Hunt (27th MA Vols), all by command of Gen. Innis N. Palmer. The excerpts from the investigation are taken from the transcripts on file at the National Archives.

Harland testified on May 14. He stated that the orders to evacuate Washington came at 11pm, April 26. The 1st NCUV was to be the first to leave aboard the "Thomas Collyer" and go to New Bern. The 1st NCUV did leave the next day with their families around dusk, except for Co L. That same day word was out among the troops and citizens that they were evacuating. Harland stated that citizens came to him in fear and he reassured them that they were absolutely not leaving although he knew otherwise. Harland claimed that townsfolk were also scared, having heard rumblings that Navy officer

Richard Renshaw, commander of the *Louisiana*, was going to "burn the town." The Confederates were very close as well.

On the 27th of April two Union soldiers were killed by a Rebel sniper who was hidden behind a stump on a higher area on the outskirts of town, near the present day hospital. Graham, who had a habit of being at the right place at the right time, was also present but ran away before the call was given, hightailing it back to Harland. Harland ordered Capt. Rowland R West of the 12th NY Cavalry to be Provost Marshall and one of West's companies to be Provost Guards. According to Harland's testimony, on the 28th he sent all the cavalry he had to New Bern by land. We will see that Graham's company, or at least he alone, did not leave that day. The 17th Mass added men as Provost Guards after looting commenced, but the stealing only became worse. Harland called the cavalry Provost Guards "useless." COs were ordered to tell the company commanders to prevent their soldiers from entering town, which did no good. What did come out of the testimonies was that in some cases, officers were joining in with their soldiers in vandalism and theft. Increasing the number of guards yet again was in vain. That evening, still the 28th of April, Lt. Pratt of Harland's staff, saw men in a locked jewelry store. Pratt only detained one before the rest escaped. It turned out they were from the 17th Mass, and the one man Pratt caught was a sergeant. When Harland left on the 29th he put Col. McChesney in command, and instructed that the bridge have its draw destroyed with axes, not fire. "Don't burn the bridge" was the order. The next day it would go from bad to worse.

Regarding the looting of the town, it is remarkable how many people knew nothing despite the chaos in the streets. By then many troops had left. The town was already in sad shape, goods lay the streets, shops broken into, and even the Masonic Hall had been entered and looted. One captain of the 1st NCUV, David Lake, told of seeing a small sailor boy breaking into the Masonic building. Lake only knew his name was Tom and he had been discharged (this was but a few weeks after the incident) and whereabouts unknown. There was no doubt that the 1st NCUV Quartermaster stores was among the first to be broken into, soldiers of all regiments were seen helping themselves. 5th RI soldiers were dividing up stolen nuts and candy right in the street, and on that last day, April 30, Capt. Wheeler's clerk spotted looters in Fowle's shop and ran them off. Acting Steward James Harvey from the *Thomas Collyer*, saw two men from Rhode Island in a shop about to break a Regulator (clock). He stopped them and the owner, Mr. Martin, asked him to take the clock and any unbroken items to New Bern.

Looting was the least of the legacy the Union left behind. There were also fires deliberately started, mainly in the Cavalry stables and kitchen. Many were extinguished but in some cases surrounding buildings were blown up to prevent the fires from spreading. Winds were high that day and though the fires were started near the river, they quickly spread away from the waterfront. Before the last troops could get clear of the town, the bridge was burned. The flames from the bridge spread back into town. After the last Union soldier was gone, Little Washington looked like a stereotypical victim of Damn Yankees and their barbarity. Looking at the notes from the investigation we can see both incompetence and deliberate destruction, as well as the possibility that the Navy had been set up in a way to take the blame. Let us look at the evidence that Graham was involved in a small plot to burn the city or was himself a committed arsonist.

It is interesting that whenever Graham went out with just his troops or was only mildly supervised, something eventually burned. In his testimony, Lt. Gill of the 12th NY

Cav stated that Co. L. left by land on the 28th. Graham probably should not have been in Little Washington on the 30th, but he was obviously still in town based on later testimony. But it may be unfair in this case to label Capt. Graham as an arsonist.

Let's deeply examine the testimonies burning of the town. Most witnesses claimed that the first fire started in one of the cavalry stables. Two privates from the 17th Mass went to the burning stables only to be run off by two officers. One private at the scene commented that this was a shame and wanted to put out the stable fire. Another officer told him it wasn't his problem and to leave it. The other witness stated that he entered the stable's kitchen area and found the two officers stacking boxes and setting them on fire. He said that this was bad, that the Rebels would see the smoke and realize the Union was evacuating. He was also told it was none of his business, but retorted that as he was on provost duty it was his business. Then one of the officers, a cavalry officer, pulled a sword and said he "would stick him." The private left and reported this to Capt. Smith. It may be easy to say to us, "Oh, that sounds like George!" But as he was so well known, and cavalry officers were all over the place, it's impossible to say that it was indeed he.

Capt. Simonds of the 17th Mass, who brought back the bodies killed by the sniper on the hill, testified that he was loading his men on board the *Thomas Collyer* to leave Little Washington and went to the dock to see to his guards on the parapets when Graham rode up and told Simonds to get on the boat, and that HE would personally see "that (Simonds's) men were relieved and the barracks burned."

Graham's own testimony states that he was with McChesney when he noticed the first fire, but later claims he was at "the building for no more than two minutes when a fire started rapidly." He stated that he helped Col. McChesney blow up buildings to prevent flames from spreading but later in McChesney's testimony, the colonel said nothing about Graham being with him, and proposed that a Rebel in civilian clothes was the arsonist trying to make Union troops "look bad." An absurd statement from Graham's own testimony quotes him as saying, with a straight face, that the Quartermaster store wasn't looted; the sutler was actually giving those shoes, clothes and goods away![40]

Col. McChesney testified before the board on the morning of May 17. He acknowledges that when he took command on the 29th only parts of the 5th RI Arty, the 15th Conn, and the 17th Mass were still in town. Yet he claims to have seen the 12th NY Cav looting the Quartermaster store and said he gave Capt. West hell, telling the captain, who had just risen after being on guard duty all night, that he could hold him personally responsible. McChesney stated he relieved the 12th with the 17th Mass, and then replaced THEM with the 15th Conn, all on the same day, despite earlier stating that the 12th was already gone. He also testified that when he took command he had a "feeling" that someone would start a fire, claiming that Capt. Wheeler, the Acting Quartermaster, had relayed to McChesney that Commander Renshaw had threatened to burn the city. McChesney said that he told Lt. Merriam of the 15th Conn to get an officer and some decent NCOs to keep watch on Renshaw. Lt. Bishop of the same unit volunteered. It was claimed that Renshaw was spotted in town and a fire broke out at a building he was near,

---

[40] In the regiment's morning reports for May 1864 Graham is indeed listed as reporting to New Bern to give his testimony but two days later he had to return because he was "ill."

but nothing tied him to any fires. McChesney continued to testify that he saw the first fire in town at the stables, never mentioning Graham being with him at the HQ when it broke out. McChesney started to embark but stopped, giving the excuse that he did not want to leave while the town was on fire, but did leave an hour later when it was reported that the Confederates has indeed spotted the flames and knew what was going on. McChesney stated that he ordered Graham to go to the USS *Louisiana*, near the dock and opposite the fortification known as "The Castle," to tell Renshaw to send boats out to destroy the bridge's draw, but *not* by fire. McChesney was some distance down the river on the way to New Bern when he spotted the bridge burning. He relayed to Renshaw to put out the fire and spotted boats going out to do just that.

Looking at the statements and accounts by others though, McChesney doesn't seem so honest. Townspeople later declared that McChesney and his men were spotted cutting up hoses so that that any fires could not be extinguished. Two soldiers from the 15th CT testified that they spotted crowds hanging around the Masonic Hall and they both asked McChesney if they could go in, to which he replied, "It's an Odd Fellows Hall, I have no objection." This apparently gave permission for that building to be pillaged and artifacts stolen and taken aboard.

Let's take a deeper look at Col. Joe McChesney before we make judgment. A telling article in a newspaper titled, The *Confederate,* tells another tale of this man and his disregard of orders.

Dated April 20, 1864, the article is actually about a Confederate captain named Alfred Stanly, brother to "fake governor Stanly." After his release from a Union prison, he returned to his home in Little Washington to find it emptied, and what was left was a mess and a traumatized wife. Of course we must take the paper's anti-Yankee stance into consideration, but even so, the article may give us plenty of insight into the town's burning.

After a "Colonel McChesson" heard that Stanly was about to be freed in an exchange, he and his men went to Stanly's home and wreaked havoc. This colonel, no doubt McChesney, as no other Union colonel had a name anywhere near McChesson besides him, ordered his men to "search the house" with an air of glee about his manner. Were "his men" some of the NCUV? In any case, they searched the house, yes. Tore open every drawer, chest, tin, box, etc and took everything. His boys even made bags out of clothing so they could haul off anything they could. The wife's clothes were taken, all of them, so that she only had left what was on her back. Other items that were being stored in Stanly's house by other ladies/widows were taken as well. Even a piano that Mrs. Stanly had sent off was stopped in the road and taken. As if taking clothes and food wasn't enough, personal items like mementos, letters, they were hauled off as well. No doubt Innis Palmer would not be pleased by such actions, but McChesney took it upon himself to punish women living alone by looting them.

McChesney had a reputation for being rather cruel in other areas. He had been accused of meting out unreasonable punishments to soldiers, and it was even said that he was fearful that some of his own men would try to kill him![41]

---

[41] Longacre, The Sharpshooters: A History of the Ninth New Jersey Volunteer Infantry, Board of Regents of the University of Nebraska, 2017

What happened to that bridge and caused much of Little Washington to be ruined was probably the result of McChesney, either sending Graham out to do his dirty work, or operating alongside Graham. Combining pieces of testimonies from witnesses, this is what appears to have happened.

On May 14, Edwin McKeever, ensign on the *Louisiana*, testified under oath that he was on board when Graham came on the dock and hailed Renshaw. McKeever overheard Graham tell Renshaw, "Col. McChesney wants you to burn the bridge." Renshaw had no reason to doubt Graham and ordered it burned. McKeever volunteered to do it.

There is more evidence that Graham told Renshaw to burn the bridge. Capt. Buttrick of the 15th Conn was called to testify. He stated that on the 30th the town was on fire, and he received orders to roll a large amount of tar into the river. In typical fashion, Graham rode up from out of the blue and told Buttrick to "hold on" and to "save enough of that tar for Capt. Renshaw to burn the bridge." Just then a gunboat approached to take some of that tar to the bridge.

Regarding the story that soldiers and citizens were in fear that the Navy man was threatening to burn the town, McChesney claimed he'd heard it from Wheeler. When Wheeler was asked about this, he stated that he heard it from McChesney, and McChesney heard it from Harland! We already know Harland said he heard this rumor from citizens. It is almost as if a seed had been planted that week to blame Renshaw for anything that might happen.

Commander Richard T. Renshaw was already respected in the US Navy. His father had been a commander, as had his brother William, who died when his ship, the *USS Westfield,* was destroyed in 1863. On Richard Renshaw's first command a small boat had been captured from the Confederates, and the crew named it the *Renshaw* in their new commander's honor. He had also married a local woman from Chocowinity, joined in matrimony by the mayor Respess of Little Washington.[42]

While it may not seem like he had any reason to burn the town, digging deeper may have revealed something that could have been burning in his mind. Besides the recent Kinston hangings, fellow Navy officer Flusser had just been killed and Renshaw had been given the *Miami* after the Little Washington hearings.

It certainly seems as if more than a few citizens and Union officers suspected the Navy man. No one could agree even under testimony as to the rumor's origin, and no one knew much about the fires and chaos going on right under their noses, but it was mentioned many times, this detail, that "Renshaw had threatened to burn the town." The burning started with McChesney's order to Graham to relay a message to Renshaw to *not* burn the bridge. What Graham actually did was the opposite. So we know who set it afire, but on whose orders? When finally asked about his message to Renshaw, his answer was that he hailed the boat and said, "Col. McChesney sends his compliments and wishes you to send a boat crew to the bridge to destroy the draw." He even acknowledged that McKeever was there, but, according to Graham, told him that they had no boats.

---

[42] The USS *Renshaw* was named for him and his elder brother, William B. Renshaw.

The million dollar question seems to be: Did Graham purposely disobey McChesney's orders or was there an "understanding" between the two men that they would burn the town, defying General Palmer's orders, defiantly not leaving anything for the Confederates coming into town? Or perhaps Renshaw was maddened with anger at Flusser's death and blamed it on Graham and McChesney, claiming they told him to burn it?

It may have been simply a case of a disreputable colonel and one of his captains, in the area, at the same time as a furious Naval officer. Add them up and you likely have a disaster. What do the regimental books say about Little Washington? Nothing. Daily reports? Not a mention of the burning. One last curious item concerning Graham does show up in those daily reports: In April's company books, for the dates of the fire, Graham is reported as leaving Little Washington. Yet, in May he is again listed as leaving the city.

It is possible he was ordered to leave, and for whatever reason was listed as such, but stayed around to take advantage of the chaos.

Whether he did this all on his own or was in cahoots with one or more people is unknown. I suspect the latter. McChesney and Wheeler appeared to have instigated the Renshaw rumor. Also, and this is speculation from knowing Graham like we now do, we imagine him questioning authority upon hearing that the town was not to be destroyed. It is not implausible that he would have thought, "Foolish, to leave the town for the rebels."

Curiously, Renshaw was not ordered to give his statement. During the testimony he had been placed in command of the USS *Miami*.[43] When the results of the investigation were published, we can imagine more than a few eyebrows were raised. Or was the Navy protecting the instigator?

The following was ordered read aloud for days to all of the regiments:

CIRCULAR ORDERS, HDQRS. DISTRICT OF NORTH CAROLINA,

New Bern, N. C., May 30, 1864.

I. Before a board of investigation, of which Colonel James W. Savage, Twelfth New York Volunteer Cavalry, is president, convened at New Bern, N. C., by virtue of Special Orders, Numbers 16, paragraph I, and Special Orders, Numbers 26, paragraph II, current series, from these headquarters, were summoned various persons, officers, soldiers, and citizens, bearing testimony relative to the facts and circumstances connected with the burning of certain portions of the town of Washington, N. C., and the pillage of that place, alleged to have been committed by certain men in the military and naval service of the United States during the late evacuation, from whose testimony the Board of Investigation deduce the following, viz:

At about 11 p. m. on the 26th of April, 1864, Brigadier-General Harland, in command at Washington, N. C., received orders to evacuate that place, and in pursuance of his instructions the post was finally abandoned about 4 p. m. on the 30th. The intended evacuation seems to have become known, or to have been generally suspected, on

---

[43] The Louisiana met a grim fate. It was used as a floating bomb by the Union in a failed attempt to blow up Fort Fisher.

Wednesday, the 27th of April. During the afternoon of that day there appears to have been instances of theft, and before morning of Thursday pillaging commenced, at first in the quartermaster's store of the First North Carolina (Union) Volunteers, which during the day became general. Government stores, sutlers' establishments, dwelling-houses, private shops, and stables, suffered alike. Gangs of men patrolled the city, breaking into houses and wantonly destroying such goods as they could not carry away. The occupants and owners were insulted and defied in their feeble endeavors to protect their property.

The influence and authority of offices, though sufficient to restrain these excesses when they were personally present, was forgotten or set at naught as soon as they were out of sight, and the sack was checked only by the lack of material to pillage, and ceased only with the final abandonment of the town. It is claimed, and may be true, that some portion of these outrages arose from a general impression that a large amount of stores and property would, upon the abandonment of the place, either be destroyed or left to fall into the hands of the enemy, but this is probably not seriously regarded by any one as a justification, or even palliation, of the utterly lawless and wanton character of the plundering.

The members of the Board, having summoned and examined all those persons within their reach who it was supposed could give any material testimony on the subject, regret that they have been able to identify so few of the individuals concerned in these violations of good order and discipline, but they are of opinion that none of the troops in Washington on the 28th of April last can reasonably claim to escape a share of the shame and odium which the history of those few days has justly caused. These were the Fifty-eighth Pennsylvania Volunteers, the Twenty-first Connecticut Volunteers, detachments of the Fifteenth Connecticut Volunteers and the Seventeenth Massachusetts Volunteers, two companies of the Fifth Rhode Island Volunteer Artillery, Ransom's New York battery, two companies of the Twelfth New York Cavalry, and the cavalry company of the First North Carolina (Union) Volunteers. Nor were these alone guilty. Sailors from the gun-boats, hands employed on the transports, negroes, and in some instances citizens, joined in the work of plunder and devastation. The Board are glad, however, to be able to record their opinion that the officers present in Washington generally, perhaps without exception, not only discountenanced, but used their best endeavors to repress, the disorder and pillage.

At 10 o'clock on the morning of the 30th, and as the last troops were about embarking, a fire broke out in some stables, which had for two days been unoccupied. The conflagration extended to adjacent buildings, and spread so rapidly as to defy all attempts to extinguish it. That this fire was designedly caused admits of little question, but the Board are unable to come to any satisfactory conclusion as to the guilty parties. Some four hours later Colonel McChesney, at that time in command of the post, sent by one of his officers a verbal order to Commander Renshaw, of the gun-boat Louisiana, then in the stream, in consequence of which that officer sent a boat's crew and set fire to the bridge across the Tar River. This fire also is supposed to have spread through the town. So far as appears in evidence, the fires which caused such serious destruction of property originated at these two points alone. Other fires were kindled, but extinguished in every instance before they had caused any damage. The commander of the post declares that he had no intention whatever of burning the bridge, but whether his instructions were carelessly given, incorrectly transmitted, or misapprehended, or willfully disregarded by the commander of the Louisiana, **the Board do not deem a matter of great importance.**
II. The findings of the Board of Investigation in this case are approved, and published for

the information of those concerned. III. The Board of Investigation, of which Colonel James W. Savage, Twelfth New Your Cavalry, is president, is dissolved.

By command of Brigadier General I. N. Palmer

Incredibly, the board deemed it unimportant as to the origin of the bridge fire, a fire that spread into the town and destroyed much of the main area. It was unimportant to know if it was willfully set, against all orders. It was unimportant to call in Renshaw for his side of the story. The whole shameful thing was written off as naughty behavior by soldiers and what did it matter that commanders were either incompetent and had no plan for evacuation, or were actually joining in the looting?

It was important enough to punish someone, and McChesney was arrested for the severe destruction of the city (lending more credence that the burning was on his hands), but later exonerated. No one was ever held to account, just entire units chastised like schoolboys. To this day locals remember the story of the little town being destroyed by Damn Yankees and, though many were indeed guilty of pillaging, only one or a few were the firebugs. Years later, despite Palmer possibly overlooking Graham's involvement, he would comment on him in a letter to another officer, writing that he was "...sorry that any weight should be given to the evidence of Captain Graham, whom I knew to be one of the most unprincipled villains in the country..."[44]

Palmer may have disliked George but he trusted him in cavalry actions. Later in the year, the Official Records show that Palmer had sent a message to Col. Thomas Amory, commanding the Sub-District of Beaufort, NC, and directed him to be on the watch for rebel activity, and to make use of "Graham's cavalry."

In that strange phenomena of what some call synchronicity, on May 12, the first day of testimonies, a Buffalo War Song was published in the New Bern Times. There is no clue to authorship other than it was written in February at Beaufort, NC. Six verses tell about avenging innocent deaths by the traitors, fighting on the land of our forefathers and defending the Republic in the swamps of Marion.[45] Some of the lines also refer, in retrospect, to nighttime looting. The first lines are:

-- *"Arise comrades, --up! The camp fires are bright,*

come gather around their embers to-night,

for day shall return, but not with the scenes,

which twilight hath left with the sunset serene."--

The third stanza is also interesting to dissect:

-- *"We know every forest and path and ravine,*

we fear not their bloodhounds, our scent is as keen.

And long before dawn a dozen or more,

---

[44] *Congressional Record: Proceedings of the United States Congress.* US Government Printing Office. 1878.
[45] Presumably Francis Marion, the "Swamp Fox."

shall land on the dusky Plutonian shore."[46]

It certainly sounds like a group of men who come out at nightfall, avenging death and wreaking havoc on the area, but more than this they claim to be very familiar with the areas. Graham had been singled out prior for his knowledge of this part of North Carolina and his band of Buffaloes lived up to the stereotype. We may never know the truth of Little Washington.

Co. L records at NARA reveal that Capt. Graham had to be reprimanded several times for failing to get his monthly books in on time, one in particular called his lack of timely bookkeeping an "embarrassment." It is amazing that he was able to get away with so much and yet continue portraying himself as a noble hero. Maybe he got away with it all because his looting and recklessness helped the Union in some way, keeping rebel partisans at bay, at least in the minds of his commanders.

Records show that George was on leave to New Bern again while Co. L was in Carolina City, this was no doubt to testify, and he returned to his company on the 19th. June saw him on sick leave again, then returning from an undisclosed location near the end of the month. He may have attended an NCUV event on the 4th of July at Fort Macon but in July his company was at Newport Barracks. He might have remained there if he was trading with the enemy. Trading with the enemy?

Col. Henry Splaine wrote in his memoirs that Graham and a few of his trusted thieves fired upon a captured blockade-runner at Bogue Sound. The guards assumed they were under enemy fire and fled, enabling Graham's bunch, perhaps dressed in CSA uniforms, to go on board to help themselves to any spoils. Splaine writes this as happening in January, but the only runner I've found that ran aground on Bogue was the *Pevensey*, on June 9, 1864. It apparently missed its turn onto the Cape Fear River and was chased by the Union blockader *New Bern* in the dark. The crew managed to get ashore save one man who stayed to explode the boiler. It was said in reports that the crew was captured by nearby cavalry troops and that about $14,000 in unnamed specie was found on them.[47] Splaine may have been recounting the story later, maybe Graham and his cavalry took Confederate uniforms from the *Pevensey*, or got hold of a large amount of cash. The Company L books from June 1864 indicate something unusual could have happened. Two days after the *Pevensey* ran aground Graham went on some type of leave claiming illness, and returning to duty two days later. In the third week of June the daily books are left blank for five days. Elsewhere, even if nothing of incident happened, that was reported as "No Adjustments." Why those days are blank is a mystery, but Splaine suspected Graham of stealing money from the *Pevensey*, and recalled that Graham had been looking for a way to hide his spoils. Was he on leave for a few days to hide anything he stole, if indeed it was his cavalry that went to Bogue that night? After those five blank days it was reported that Capt. Graham "returned." Where he returned from is unlisted.

The problem with the legend is...the *Pevensey* had no gold/specie. After an exhaustive search, I have found no other grounded runner in that area in that time frame. Splaine may have heard a rumor and spread it in that regiment's history. Over time it has

---

[46] Was the writer a fan of Edgar Allan Poe? This may be a nod to *The Raven*, and its line "Night's Plutonian Shore."
[47] New Bern Times, June 15, 1864.

become so blown out of proportion that it's almost comical. I was notified of "a website" claiming that 'ol Georgie obtained the gold by robbing UNION gold that was stored in Swansboro! Highly unlikely, since that town was Confederate held. Naturally, the mysterious website cannot be located. Graham's gold probably came from a Newberne merchant, formerly in the CSA, and before that, gold hunting in California.

His company was preparing to replace the 9th VT at Newport Barracks. The area was still not entirely safe for Union regiments to wander. The 9th VT had engaged in fighting since the past winter, with several deaths. Captain Samuel Kelly of the 9th took some forty men across the White Oak River to Swansboro several members of the 7th NC Cavalry who were at an outpost.[48] The White Oak still served as a border of sorts between Union and Confederate, as it did two years previously when Graham had his engagement up at Young's Crossroads.

The 9th VT was sending companies A, F, H, and K to New Bern with the rest to follow later. They were kept busy creating a cemetery for those who had fallen since their arrival. The cemetery consisted of a cedar fence and "headstones" made of the same wood.[49] When Graham and his men arrived at Newport Barracks they found no shops. No tree lined streets. Mosquitoes and wood ticks replaced any comforts. Oh, and there was little chance of getting drunk. The North Carolina *Times* made up a song in parody of the "Charge of the Light Brigade" titled "Forward the Tight Brigade," making humorous the cities the Union occupied.[50] Despite the proximity to the city, and the situation not being as horrendous as parts of Virginia and its battles, there were still sobering moments. Executions taking place near the Union camps were not rare. It must have been a sight to see fellow soldiers, caught deserting, sitting on their own coffins awaiting a firing squad, with a music band present no less.

It was a rainy Independence Day at Fort Macon in 1864. The 1st NCUV held a large celebration with formal invitations, and Graham likely attended. Years later, a man calling himself James Hooper claimed to have been not just a boyhood friend of Graham's, but wrote that he was at Fort Macon when Graham made a speech. Graham was quoted as saying he was no speaker or writer, "but give me a sabre and I will leave my mark!"[51]

He almost left a mark on Capt. Henry Splaine, who was learning to hate Graham. When Splaine, of the 17th Mass, was ordered by Gen. Palmer to take over the area at Newport Barracks that had been used by the 9th VT, he found Graham and his boys defiant that they wanted that area for themselves. Graham had removed the Vermont soldiers' huts and dumped them around the area, not even waiting for them to leave. Splaine told Graham to put back those huts that the 17th Mass had been ordered by Palmer to have that area. Splaine continued to tell Graham that he would actually read Palmer's orders to him, and asked again to replace the huts and material, kindly volunteered his own men to do the work to save Graham embarrassment. Instead of doing the right thing, Graham attempted to pull a pistol on Splaine, a fellow captain. Splaine was

---

[48] Wickman, *We Are Coming Father Abra'am, The History of the 9th Vermont Volunteer Infantry 1862-1865*. Schroeder Publications 2005
[49] Ibid.
[50] August 23, 1864.
[51] James Hooper remains unknown, as do his boyhood friend stories.

quicker and pulled his out first. Splaine told Graham to send his men off and they would settle it between themselves. Graham did order his men away but they remained, enjoying this show, causing Splaine to comment on how undisciplined Graham's gang was. He sent his Massachusetts men off and they obeyed, but one of Graham's Buffaloes approached Splaine who saw he was alone and surrounded by the scraggly mob. He had the nerve to cuss at the officer and threaten him. After falling over a log the unruly jerk wandered off. Graham still refused to leave the area, defying Palmer's orders. After a stare-down in which both men held their guns, Splaine's men rushed back sensing his danger. Graham recognized that he could not bully this man, and also saw he was outnumbered, and gave up. According to his memoirs, Splaine said that Graham was brave, yes, brave enough to bully and fight other officers, even those outranking him, and beat a few so badly that they had to go on leave.

He also apparently got away with so much because when he did capture enemy horses and prisoners he did such a good job that his superiors overlooked his personality. Then again, Splaine was certainly wrong about a ship-robbing, gold-thieving incident, so who knows what actually transpired that day.

Splaine had many stories of Graham, which were published long after the war.[52] In August they gave chase to a rebel scout known as Nickerson near Young's Crossroads. Graham was eager to fire upon and kill anyone without a second thought, and, after finding a trap set by the Confederates, Graham questioned a Sgt. Perkins, 6th GA Cavalry[53], captured by the 17th Mass and Graham's cavalry. Graham wanted the NCO shot on the spot but Splaine intervened and Graham, secretly trading with a former Confederate, admonished Splaine, asking him if he was siding with a "damned rebel."

The loose type of record keeping regarding his actions occurs again in August, as he is listed as returning from an unnamed location, and the same yet again on September 2. Splaine wrote about another expedition with Graham in August, which could explain the records showing Graham coming back from parts unknown. As Splaine recounts, they were all bored at Newport Barracks. He took Graham and some of Co. L with him into enemy territory by going across the Pamlico Sound. At that time the area was not very populated.

It wasn't a quick trip but they eventually found themselves along Smith Creek, likely the present area of Orient. The men found a mansion and asked a woman for water, telling her that they were an advance party, "just in case." They next wandered to a farm where they obtained watermelons from a woman only identified as Miss Betsey. As they sat around eating the melon Splaine kept watch on the property and noticed a mounted Confederate officer approaching. Keeping out of sight, they watched the officer unlock the gate and ride in, effectively locking himself inside an area where he and his horse could not easily escape. Splaine and the others took the man's pistol as the prisoner said he recognized Splaine. It turned out that his father, Jabez Bell, lived near Newport Barracks and Splaine knew the man. The Confederate, who gave his name as Capt. George Bell, said he almost shot Splaine while the latter was visiting Jabez Bell in the past but thought it would be outright murder. The Union men decided to take him back as a prisoner but

---

[52] Kirwin, *Memorial History of the Seventeenth Regiment, Massachusetts Volunteer Infantry in the Civil War*.
[53] Search of records has turned up nothing on this man.

would let him stop and see his family near Newport Barracks, of course they would all enjoy a good meal while there.

Meanwhile Miss Betsey had fled the house on foot to get help. Splaine and Graham decided to get back to the boat, hoping it was still where they left it. They had ordered a black man to watch it and given him a weapon to do so. The boat with its sailor and guard were still there and they boarded without the horse. Bell had been interrogated along the long ride back across the Sound, and told Splaine to stop gallivanting around in the Newport area or they would come to grief. "Don't tempt the goddess too far" was the quote Splaine remembered. They stopped at a farmhouse and had a destitute woman cook breakfast for them. Bell had many letters in his pockets that were intended for Confederate families, including one for the very woman that was making their meal. Splaine felt bad for the woman whose husband was away because she and her children were hungry. After reading her husband's letter he gave it to her and paid her for her trouble.

The group finally settled for the night in a small building with a black family, sleeping with Bell between them. The family was told that they would be killed if the prisoner made a move. Despite this, Bell waited until Splaine and Graham were fast asleep, made his way to a window and threatened the family, who obviously couldn't sleep, and jumped through the window. The noise awoke Graham and Splaine who stumbled about in a sleepy stupor to find the soldiers outside asleep on their watch. Bell had escaped.

The men went to Jabez Bell's home anyway once they reached Newport Barracks. The escapee's sister accused the Union men of killing her brother, but Splaine assured her that Americans don't kill but fight honorably, and that George had truly escaped. Sister Alice was clapping her hands in joy and admitted she liked being called a "Little Rebel" by the Unionists.[54] The story may have a grain of truth but also sounds exaggerated by Splaine.

One Splaine-story that I was able to track was his relationship to this ex-Confederate merchant. According to the 17th Mass he was trading Union army equipment for "Confederate gold." Capt. Splaine intercepted a letter to Graham from a Confederate, "Capt. McDuffie," via a middleman. The stranger was attempting to get this message to Graham on Trading Day at Newport Barracks, but was a day early. Splaine was suspicious when he saw the man shoving something in his pocket and demanded the items. Among a bundle of letters was a note to Graham, which the stranger tried again to hide. The man said that some farmer asked him to get the letter to Capt. Graham at Newport Barracks. Splaine later read the letter while back at camp after running off the messenger.

In the letter McDuffie wrote to Graham about a plan they had cooked up whereby Graham would get Union army supplies to McDuffie, and McDuffie would pay Graham in gold. Early the next morning, Trading Day, Splaine saw Graham already at the post

---

[54] No records found for a Capt. George Bell in the North Carolina rosters, but a George T. Bell was in the 1st NC Artillery (10th State Troops). He enlisted in Carteret County, and was discharged in 1862. Jabez has been transcribed as Jabey in some files, this leading to confusion. Jabez Bell may have had connections to confirmed spy Josiah Fisher Bell of Morehead City, and who was part of a plan to blow up nearby lighthouses. I have found no Alice Bell fitting the age group.

chatting with the very man Splaine had taken the letter from and had warned to stay away. Graham sensed that Splaine knew his dangerous secret. This incident must have been later in 1864, as Splaine claimed that he avoided traveling alone with Graham as he simply did not trust him at all now, and that Graham was friendlier to Splaine after this. Maybe knowing that a person had info on him that could get him hanged was what it took to make Graham less antagonistic.

Regarding the Confederate trader McDuffie, Splaine left a clue. McDuffie had a wife with the maiden name of Jones, whose sister was known among the NCUV as "Graham's adopted wife." In 19th century parlance, an adopted wife most likely meant that she was his wife in every sense of the word but not legally married, or possibly a fiancée.

After many dead-end leads, it has been discovered that Capt. McDuffie was actually former Lieutenant Samuel S. Duffy, living in New Bern, and served with the 2nd Artillery under the 36th NC State Troops. His company, unattached, was the "first" version of Company G, aka Leecraft's Company.

Duffy, an Irish immigrant, was married on September 20, 1849 to Elizabeth Fisher Jones, daughter of prominent merchant and hotelier John Fisher Jones, Esq and Rebecca Alice Ward Jones.[55] Duffy's family consisted of physicians and druggists, while Samuel operated a store in New Bern.

After the war, Duffy became active in auctioneering. Let it be noted, however, that this did not necessarily make Duffy a bad person for "trading with Yankees." It is not known what army supplies Graham was trading for gold, but it is likely that they were medical supplies. This makes Graham look even worse for taking medicines away from his own men and pocketing the money. What is known is that Duffy's wife Elizabeth had two younger sisters, Mary Fisher Jones, and Josephine Jones, who only shows up in the 1860 census. As it turns out, Josephine was indeed the "adopted wife." Did Graham meet her first and, for whatever reason, told her he could get goods to her brother-in-law, Sam Duffy? Could he have been mixed up in a spy network, unwittingly or not?

Early in September, another enemy was to hit New Berne: Yellow Fever.

Sources were claiming that shipment of clothing from New York had been contaminated and brought the fever to town. An aide to General Palmer died, as did Col. Amory of the 17th Mass. Men from the 27th Mass served as nurses. The epidemic reached such a point that the only people who seemed to be on the streets were funeral processions. Homes were checked at least once daily for victims. 27th Mass chaplain John Hill Rouse served as clergyman to many of these corteges. Rouse, in his fifties, was well known and much loved in the city for his kind manner.

October was quiet, mainly due to the Yellow Fever epidemic, and Graham is listed as being on sick leave in November, but probably not from the fever, for in December his company went to Plymouth for a large attempt to raid the interior area.

A couple of items of note are in the Company L books for December 1864. Each day in the monthly books is filled in, even if only a few words. But the days of December 7-27 are blank. It was noted that Graham and the entire company went to Plymouth but the

---

[55] Wilmington, NC *Chronicle*, Oct 17, 1849.

reason is not known. After the entry for the 6th, noting the Plymouth sojourn, someone had written the curious line "When this (*illegible*) over remember me." Did the company fear they would not return?

Private Patrick Norris, who joined the company earlier in the year, was given Christmas furlough. Though it is unknown how many men Graham gave holiday furloughs to, we can imagine many wanted them and were refused. Did Norris have a relative who was victim of Yellow Fever? Graham made a gracious gesture to Norris at the time, who wouldn't forget. Despite Graham's forays into scoundrel territory, he was noted by a few acquaintances after his death as having been fully capable of having a generous nature.

On the 9th of December, Graham's cavalry, along with cavalry from the 3rd and 12th NY, waited for the rest of the forces. They, along with the 27th Mass, artillery from the 2nd Mass Heavy Artillery, 85th NY, 16th CT, and 101st and 103rd PA, and 9th NJ were under command of the 2nd Mass's Col. James Frankle. Graham commanded the cavalry. As they reached Gardner's Creek Bridge (at present day Jamesville, NC) he ran into a large number of Confederates and found himself outnumbered. The rebels were planning to set the bridge on fire with turpentine when Graham and the rest of the cavalry companies found them, and, realizing he needed more men, Graham got a message to Col. James Stewart of the 9th, the message quoted as "Come up and brush the butternuts out of the path!" Stewart and his men responded noisily, running off the Confederates before they could burn the site.

A few days later Col. Stewart and troops surprised the 68th NC while they were sleeping on the road near Fort Branch.[56] Further in, after the 68th was captured, Stewart's men lost out at more captures. Owing to some disorganization in communications, the Confederates along the Tarboro Road managed to make their escape, chased by Graham and the rest of the cavalry. More skirmishing took place later, Stewart's horse being among the losses, and word spreading that Col. Frankle was missing from where he promised he would be, and many men opining that had Frankle been where he said he would be, many more Confederates would have been killed or captured at this area known as Rainbow Bluff. Frankle was deemed incompetent of the task. One objective of the mission at Rainbow Bluff was to find and destroy another ironclad ram that, according to rumor, was being built.

On the 12th Graham and a few men noticed some Confederates "acting strangely" along a road, and assumed they wanted to surrender. Graham waved a dirty handkerchief at them. Upon approaching them the Yankees found that, not only were the rebels refusing to surrender, they were warned of a huge force under Longstreet approaching and that the Unionists would never see Union lines again. It was untrue but it scared Graham and Stewart enough that they retreated.[57]

Halfway through the first month of 1865 Graham was on a few days leave of absence, and the in middle of February they took out a Confederate camp near Greenville before moving into town itself, where Graham and his men raided a Confederate commissary and took Commissary General Major William E. Demille[58] prisoner.

---

[56] Near Hamilton, NC
[57] Drake, James M, *The History of the Ninth New Jersey Veteran Vols: A Record of its Service*.
[58] Grandfather of Hollywood producer Cecil B. DeMille.

Graham and his bandits preferred to find less dangerous targets wherever they could, as a black man named Jacob Cherry, found out that month. According to another claim in the Southern Claims Commission files, Cherry named Graham as the man who stole his horse. Between the 17th and 22nd of February, Graham and Co. L were listed at being in New Bern, but apparently the Graham wanted another so-called expedition.

Cherry testified that he had earned some money in January and bought a horse from a freed slave. The following month Cherry saw not only his own horse taken but many horses from other civilians in the area. He was himself farming land belonging to a family named Brown. He had no Confederate ties; indeed he had a brother in the Union Army. During the morning of the incident Cherry was plowing a field belonging to Benjamin Brown when he saw Graham's company ride in. Cherry knew that they were in the area for the purpose of taking every horse they could find. Someone ordered the man to bring the horse over to him, and when Cherry explained that it was his property, the soldier obviously doubted that the black man owned it. Cherry wasn't giving up so easily. He rode that horse into town alongside the soldiers who took him directly to Graham at a headquarters building. Graham stated that so many colored people were claiming property he could not be sure of believing him. He then made the same empty promise to Cherry as he did to Harrison the previous autumn. If Cherry would go to New Bern, he would get that horse back to him or give him another horse. The horse was a young and pregnant. Cherry was not able to get to New Bern until July, where he found Graham still in town after the war. Graham just shrugged and said that Cherry was too late; that he had no horses to give him and that they had been turned in. A witness, John Bartlett, wrote that he was in the area during Graham's horse raid. Bartlett, working at the Confederate Commissary in Greenville, knew Cherry and knew the details of his acquisition of the horse. He was also present when he saw Cherry ride into town on that horse with a Union cavalryman. Bartlett said he had no idea why Federal troops were in the area as no Confederates were left, unless they knew about the Commissary and/or wanted to raid farms, saying that they did burn the Commissary and take every horse they could find around town. He also emphasized that the mare was quite valuable by that time, as horses were scarce and this one was with foal. Cherry was eventually paid $150 for the loss. Of course, there is a quirk ending to this story: One of the witnesses for Cherry was William E. Demille, the same person earlier captured at that Commissary, and who no doubt enjoyed testifying in some way against Graham.

Early in March 1865 Graham was on duty away from camp. He was involved in a skirmish at Gum Swamp, with no reported injuries.[59] The roads to the area were very bad, owing to recent storms. The Union found not only muddy, swampy roads, but also many trees down on the way from New Bern. John Hedrick wrote in his letters that he was in New Bern on the 8th and found almost no troops. According to him the NCUV held Macon and they were concentrated from Carolina City to Beaufort on their way to Kinston.[60]

While Gen. Sherman made his way to Goldsboro, Graham's Cavalry wound up at the Battle of Wise's Forks near Kinston. Some sources identify Co. L as an Independent Troop of North Carolina Cavalry during the battle. This was a somewhat overlooked but very important battle in the Civil War. It looked bad for the Union for a short time that spring of 1865 in North Carolina, but, thanks to reinforcements, Gen. Bragg would have to

---

[59] Pittsburgh Daily Commercial, Mar 15, 1865
[60] Hedrick, *Letters from a North Carolina Unionist*, (North Carolina Dept. Of Cultural Resources 2001).

withdraw at the end. Sherman's army had fought at Bentonville and hooked up with Schofield near Goldsboro. Graham hadn't seen anything like this since his Goldsboro heroics in 1862. Graham and his company were sent out with artillery to guard the Neuse Road. He fought alongside the 132nd NY Infantry, driving the enemy back to Wise's Forks.

Graham later claimed to have delivered a message from Gen. Couch to Gen. Sherman, because he'd "found no one else capable of doing it."[61] Graham was mentioned by name in the *Daily Tribune* out of New Bern. On Mar 19 he was scouting about four miles outside of Goldsboro and found Confederates in the area (possibly at Cox's Bridge). This would have been in the late morning because a message was sent to Sherman from Gen. O. O. Howard shortly after 1:00pm informing Sherman that a scout had returned from reconnoitering before Goldsboro and found a crossing held by rebels.

As for the message Graham delivered from Couch, this is still a mystery. On the same morning that Graham found the rebels near Goldsboro, Schofield was sending reports to Sherman about the enemy at Cox's Bridge about supply boats arriving, as well as notes about pushing forward to Goldsboro. In any case, Graham claims it took him less than eighteen hours to deliver it to Sherman, giving researchers guessing opportunities and routes. Also, on the 19th, according to the Official Records, Couch was sending/receiving messages from Wherry, with Wherry emphasizing that he wanted Graham's company to remain where it was. Whatever was in that message, it is notable that Graham, ordered to continue scouting, found no other man "capable" of delivering the Sherman Message and left his command to do it himself. The Raleigh *Daily Conservative* ran updates, playing guessing games as to Sherman's whereabouts, as well as Schofield's. In early April it was reported that they, along with Terry, were in hourly communication. Whether Graham actually met Sherman may never be known.

At the end of March Graham was still on reconnaissance duty near Goldsboro and Company L reported a gain of two horses captured from the enemy on the reports of the 27th.

Graham made the papers again when The Raleigh *Daily Conservative* mentioned him on April 4th regarding his reconnoitering the Rebel positions, and the Cleveland *Daily Leader* named Graham as one of the "1st North Carolina mounted rangers" who had captured "1600 rebels within the past few months" and would probably "bring in the rest of Bragg's army."[62]

During the last few weeks of the war, the Reverend Rouse, still in charge of Christ Church on Pollock St, publicly complained that people were using the church grounds as both a trash pit and cattle yard, as locals (or soldiers?) were letting their cows wander the grounds, as well as toss used bottles in the area.[63]

In May three of Graham's men accompanied him for special duty for two days and nights, returning the day of Lincoln's death. The reason for this duty was not given in the daily books.[64]

---

[61] Graham's Personal Files, National Archives, Washington DC.
[62] Cleveland *Daily Leader*. April 5, 1865.
[63] New Bern *Times*. April 7, 1865.
[64] Records of the 1st NCUV, Series: Regimental and Company Books of the Civil War Vol Organizations 1861-1867, RG 94: Records of the Adjutant General's Office, National Archives, Washington DC.

Afterwards Graham and some enlisted men returned to the scene of a crime when they went on unspecified duty in Little Washington, with over twenty more men added to that duty. They all returned on the last day of May, and June's books show nothing remarkable, mainly men going off and on sick call. The books end on June 24th, 1865. For May, the bookkeeping ends with this statement at the bottom of the page:

That Is Finished

Capt. Graham was not officially mustered out when he wrote to Stanton in Washington, DC, asking for a commission in the Regular Army. Dated June 18, the letter has Graham briefly listing his service since "the beginning of the Rebellion," and his rank of Captain in Oct 1863. He enclosed documents to enable, as he puts it, Stanton to "fully understand his services." Graham gives the following synopsis of his military career in the letter:

-- *"I was mustered into the United States service as a 1st Lieut of the 24th N.Y. Ind Battery at Albany N.Y. 1st Dec 1861. Embarked for Washington D.C. the same day and remained in that place until April 1862. When I embarked with the Battery for New Bern No Ca during my service with the Battery I participated in the following engagements: viz White Oak River, Gum Swamp, Kinston, Whitehall, and Goldsboro No Ca at the latter place I was wounded. On or about the 1st of Feb 1863 I was transferred at my own request to the 3d N.Y. Vol Cav. I served with that Regt three months and was once wounded on out Post duty and participated in the following engagements viz Blounts Mills and the Siege of Little Washington No Ca. On or about the 1st of May 1863 I was promoted to Captain and ordered to the command of an Independent Company of Cavalry in which capacity I served until the close of the War. During my service with the last named Co my duties were of the most arduous kind in consequence of the Co being use (sic) exclusively for Scouts. Part of the results of these duties were the capture of three Companies of Cav five of Infantry and one Field Piece with equipments complete, als over two Thousand head of animals In March 1865 I captured the Town of Greenville N.C. at that time used by the enemies as a Depot for supplies and (illegible) over one Million dollars worth of Commissary Stores. The value here stated are those given me by the Post Commissary whom I also captured at the same time. In May 1865 I participated in the Engagements at Wises Fork and in the Front of Kinston. While in front of Kinston I received orders from Maj. Gen Couch – Commanding 23d A.C. to secure a man who would volunteer to deliver a message to Maj. Gen Sherman. I failed to find a man and attempted it myself which I accomplished delivering the dispatch within 18 hours from the time it was delivered to my passing through the Rebel Gen Braggs lines. I respectfully refer to the enclosed documents which show to some extent the nation of the service I have performed.*

I am Gentleman Army

Your Obedt Servant G W Graham" --

The war may have been finished but George Wallace Graham was not. He had a few more lives left.

Before the 1st NCUV was officially mustered out of service the New Bern *Times* wrote of a horse race near Camp Palmer. Soldiers and townsfolk had races at the old track, and of course "the most interesting race" was between Graham and a Mr. Garrettson. Garrettson's horse was in the lead for a time but when Graham's horse, not accustomed to racing and became unmanageable, Garretson had to pull back his reins and slow down. Nearing the judges Graham's horse showed signs of wearing down, running off of the track completely. The locals ate it up. Another event was reported with Graham and his horses at a race, with the *Times* pointing out what was unusual for "gatherings of this kind:" everybody was sober.

Actually New Yorkers lapped up the antics of Graham. He was mentioned in the Brooklyn *Daily Eagle*[65] for being involved in a mock fight in the streets of New Bern, with his unit being named by the paper as "Captain Graham's famous company of Mounted Rifles."

Though Co. L mustered out on June 27, 1865, the infamous Capt. Graham was still in the area until at least as late as September, spending his time and money on horse racing and no doubt enjoying the company of Josephine Jones and her family at her home. The Raleigh Daily Standard made note in July of "Captain Graham's notorious cavalry" being allowed to keep their horses. Horse racing aside he wasted no time gathering paperwork and recommendations to apply for a commission in the Regular Army. He had a backup plan in case his desire for a commission was turned down.

Many soldiers stayed in New Berne for one reason or another. The town had reason to celebrate that summer. No matter anyone's opinion on the war, it was over, and the country was ready to celebrate its birthday. Ads ran in the New Berne papers for the upcoming July 4th celebrations. Patriotic songs by military bands, picnics, and church events were held. Chaplain Rouse, so much appreciated by citizens during the Yellow Fever epidemic, held a sermon at the Episcopal Church on Pollack St.

The New Bern *Times* ran notices in their mail columns that Graham had letters to collect as late as September 30th, including a package from the Office of the Quartermaster General at Raleigh.

What he may not have known was that paperwork had been drawn up to promote Maj. Oscar Eastman to lieutenant colonel, due to McChesney's resignation. This would have pushed Graham to Major. It was turned down since they had been mustered out and no rank was made retroactive.[66]

As for the flags and standards of the NCUV, they have been noted missing by many Civil War historians. As far as anyone knows they disappeared in 1870. Governor William W Holden, later impeached mostly because of his hatred of the KKK and fondness for the Union, held a ceremony that year to bring those flags, as well as others, to the

---

[65] June 5, 1865.
[66] Reports of Committees: 30th Congress, 1st Session – 48th Congress, 2nd Session." U.S. Congress.

Capitol building in Raleigh.[67] A guard of honor in ceremonial dress delivered the flags, which were placed in the Executive Office. A description was given as follows:

> - Both of the flags were made of fine silk bunting. The United States flag is badly damaged, but the outlines are still intact. The state colors, however, were less fortunate, and the blue field, with a few of the semi-circle of stars, is alone distinguishable, the flag having been almost destroyed by shot and shell.

Graham is again mentioned in this article about the flags. It is claimed that his company captured four times their number of soldiers, and twice their number of horses, and declaring that on one occasion in Greenville, 100 enemies were captured.

Graham returned to New York via one of the steamers that departed from the Gaston House and awaited notice from Washington regarding his application. He no doubt impressed people at Saratoga Springs with money in his pockets to take to the horse races. At Saratoga, later in 1865, G. W. Graham was racing his horse "Greyhound," brought from Virginia, at least on the first race. Graham was a tall muscular man, so it was reported that he had a young boy ride Greyhound in the second.[68] In December, after the letter offering him a commission arrived and he traveled to Washington for an exam and oath, he went back to New Bern.

A letter from Graham to the Army is in the microfilmed files of his military records at NARA. In it he asks for a delay in reporting to Kansas for personal affairs. He does not tell the Army the reason: he was getting married. His backup seemed to have been marrying into a prominent family. Whether he was using them or making a goodhearted attempt to lead a straight, civilian life is unknown. He didn't have to return to North Carolina to marry Josephine but did so anyway.

In December New Bern was buzzing. Contemporary newspapers give us an idea of what was on citizens' minds that first Christmas after the war ended. Columns about the abolishment of slavery ran alongside stories of local "darkies" intended to be humorous.

AQM Wheeler was still in town asking that all government horses loaned to locals for farming use be returned by January 8th, with a sale of those same animals the next day.[69] Bars were warned that if they served intoxicating beverages to soldiers the military had the power to close them down.[70]

Samuel S. Duffy was now advertising his license as an auctioneer to drum up business. He was about to have a new in-law.

Mail for "Mrs. Josie Graham" was awaiting pickup on the 23rd of December at the post office. It was likely gifts or greetings in response to engagement announcements.

On Christmas Eve, 1865, Capt. George W. Graham, USV, married Josephine Jones in New Bern, with 27th Massachusetts Chaplain Rouse officiating.[71]

---

[67] Raleigh Weekly Standard, June 16, 1869.
[68] Burlington Weekly Free Press, Oct 6, 1865.
[69] New Bern *Times*. Dec 23, 1865.
[70] New Bern *Times*. Dec 25, 1865.
[71] New York *Evening Post*. Oct 26, 1866.

Her groom kept the marriage quiet for many years. There seem to be no wedding announcements in local papers; indeed only one was discovered in the Oct 26, 1866 edition of the New York *Evening Post*, with few details. No record is in the Craven County marriage index either. This is where more Graham-style oddities become apparent. Why would he return to marry her unless he truly cared for her or needed some connections? Without giving away spoilers, we will see he quickly turned on her. Why?

The reader will let me conjecture for a moment. However Graham met Duffy and his sister-in-law Josephine, she had affection for him. It may never be known why he traveled back to North Carolina, married Josephine, then left for Kansas, with the apparently abandoning her. One possibility is that he was treated well by the prosperous Jones and Duffy families, if they had a different motive. If he was somehow equipping the local Confederate side with medicines or equipment, he could have been nothing more than a useful idiot. He, on the other hand, may have seen himself as making money off of locals or even thinking of marrying into a prominent family in case he was turned down for regular Army service. If he was aware of the family's possible connection to spies, he may have thought HE was getting the goods on THEM. Possibly he returned to New Bern and found himself not useful anymore and looked down upon as a damn Yankee ruffian. What is strange is that the marriage was in New York papers as being in New Bern, but the no actual records exist in Craven or surrounding counties. Checking New York records proved a waste of time as well. The thought occurred that it might have been an elopement, perhaps the Jones family disapproved but seeing that Josie was receiving mail with her married name it doesn't seem likely.

Was Duffy actually in a local spy ring? Looking at marriage and birth records of the Jones family uncovered some very interesting bits. Josephine's father John Fisher Jones gained his middle name from his mother Elizabeth Fisher, an aunt of Josiah Fisher Bell, known Confederate spy involved with blowing up lighthouses at Cape Lookout. Emeline Pigott, the famous female spy, was connected to the Bells. More about Josiah Fisher Bell: his mother was Mary Polly Fisher. His wife was Susan Benjamin Leecraft, her brother being commander of the company Duffy had been in. Around ten years earlier, an announcement was posted in the New Bern *Weekly News* asking for information concerning a lost check payable to Josephine's father John, signed by Josiah Fisher Bell. The poster was Henry Clay Jones, a relative who would succumb in 1864 to Yellow Fever, and was chastised by Confederate papers for the heinous act of practicing law in New Bern during its occupation. Some pointed out that the former secessionist was a louse for "helping Yankees." Who Henry's clients were is unknown. Also, in 1857, the Beaufort *Journal* advertised a lot for sale on Turner Street, near a new female seminary, and occupied by John Fisher Jones. Interested people were instructed to contact Capt. E.W. Pigott.[72]

There was definitely some type of spy ring between New Bern and Carteret County. A local woman, Mary F. Chadwick, herself part of the same Bell family was a go-between for Josiah Fisher Bell and Col. Whitford in New Bern.[73] At least one shop in New Bern might have been a place for messages to be exchanged.

---

[72] Beaufort Journal. July 22, 1857.
[73] McKean, Brenda Chambers, *Blood and War on my Doorstep Vol 1* (Xlibris Corp, 2011).

Benjamin Leecraft, brother-in-law to Josiah Fisher Bell, was commander of the company Duffy had been in, Company G of the 2nd NC Artillery, 36th State Troops. Several Bells were in this company as well. Many were released early in 1862, some on the orders of General Gatlin. No records state why, other than hints that they may have been put under actual CSA command. No one can say whether locals were brought on as citizen-spies or not. But one more oddity was discovered: Jabez Bell, the man Splaine and Graham knew and visited, was also related to Graham's fiancée.

None of this actually proves that it included Graham's new in-laws. But it is interesting that Graham managed to become ingratiated with relatives of known spies.

Whatever time he spent in New Bern after marrying Josephine must have been short. On the 30th of December he had mail awaiting pickup in the Wilmington post office. Josephine may have went with him next, whether he went back to New York or Washington DC in preparation for his next assignment, as she had mail left behind in New Bern at the beginning of January 1866.

By sheer coincidence (or did the Cosmos have a sense of humor?), the New Year in New Bern brought an aptly named play to the local theater: *The Married Rake*.

```
Friday, October 26, 1866.

Wed. Oct. 24, Ch. of Incarnation, Rev. Henry E. Mont-
gomery   William E. Beames to Frances B dau of R G H
Huntington, all of this City.

Oct. 25, Rev. William Wilder of Phila.  Henry M Gowing
of Bklyn to Lillie E Irving of Crosbyville, Pa.

Newbern, N.C. Dec. 24, Rev. J.H. Rouse, Capt. George W
Graham of Crown Point NY to Josephine Jones dau of
John F of Newbern.
```

October 26, 1866 edition of the New York *Evening Post*. Marriage announcement notes Graham's marriage the previous December.

MARRIED.

WYAMES—HUNTINGTON—On Wednesday, October 7th, at the Church of the Incarnation, by the Rev. Henry E. Montgomery, D. D., William E. Besman to Frances B., daughter of H. G. H. Huntington, Esq., all of this city. 13

DOWING—IRVING—On the 25th inst., at the residence of the bride's father, by the Rev. William Wilder, of Philadelphia, Henry M. Dowing, of Brooklyn, N. Y., to Lillie E. Irving, of Crosbyville, Pa. 21

GRAHAM—JONES—In Newbern, N. C., on the 24th December, 1862, by the Rev. J. Hill Evans, Captain George W. Graham, U. S. V., of Crown Point, N. Y., to Miss Josephine Jones, daughter of John F. Jones, Esq., of Newbern, N. C.
Washington papers please copy. 19

JOHNES—FOULKE—On the 26th instant, by the Rev. R. Y. Chase, of St. Matthias Church, Philadelphia, Arthur Johnes, of this city, to Margaret, daughter of the late William Foulke, of Philadelphia. 11

PEABODY—PINGREE—In Salem, Mass., on the 23d inst., at the East Church, by the Rev. Mr. Bonne, Joseph Peabody to Anna Perkins, daughter of the late Hon. David Pingree, all of Salem. 23, 24—6

SPERRY—LEONARD—On Wednesday, October 24, at St. Paul's M. E. Church, by Rev. Cyrus D. Foss, assisted by Rev. J. L. G. McKown, John L. Sperry and Sarah F., daughter of William Leonard, Esq., all of this city. 14

Announcement of marriage. Best quality I could locate. New York *Evening Post*.

Buffalo Soldier Part II

Graham had been offered a commission as a 1st Lieutenant in the newly formed 10th Cavalry, headquartered at Fort Leavenworth, KS.

He traveled to Washington, DC for a medical exam and to take the oath, as well as Cavalry instruction. On Nov 22 he signed his oath in DC, with the surgeon's certificate giving his health as "physically competent to serve as a cavalry officer" and signed on Dec 5, 1866 in Washington DC. Graham himself provided his signature under the statement acknowledging as laboring under no mental or physical disability. This was after he requested to Washington the return of his recommendations, one of which was signed by U. S. Grant. He would carry this assortment of references with him for the rest of his life.

The 10th Regiment of Cavalry was approved on July 28, 1866. Six new regiments were made up of black soldiers with white officers: the 9th and 10th Cavalry, and the 38th, 39th, 40th, and 41st Infantry.

Benjamin Grierson, renowned cavalry commander during the Civil War, was in charge of the 10th, and was one of the first people Graham met upon arriving at Leavenworth. The 10th would be without a fully organized staff until 1867.

On March 26, 1867 George Wallace Graham wrote and signed his acknowledgement of a receipt of the commission of 1st Lieutenant at Fort Leavenworth and sent it off to the Adjutant General.

Leavenworth in 1867 was already a busy place. Fort Leavenworth had been established many years earlier, and the town saw many people and soldiers pass through, more so than Kansas City. The Oregon and Santa Fe Trails brought still more people through the city, so many that ruts from the countless wagons are still easily seen in one of the hills on Fort Leavenworth near the Missouri River. The namesake of the famous Harvey Houses, Fred Harvey, lived in Leavenworth and his mansion is still standing. Not long after Graham arrived in Kansas, the controversial Union General "Bloody Jim" Lane committed suicide, shocking the area and country.

Officers at that time were paid about $150 per month, not including anything extra supplied. However, getting paid each month was rare on the Frontier; sometimes pay wouldn't arrive for months. In the field a soldier had no need for money but if they were in or near cities they wanted their pay to spend on books, tobacco, and of course, liquor. Grierson's wife Alice Kirk Grierson wrote in her memoirs that in April Graham was in Kansas City and ordered back to inspect a number of horses that had arrived at Fort Leavenworth.[74] During the spring of 1867 Graham may have had his eye on a promotion. Graham was indeed promoted to Captain on account of a vacancy. The War Dept. sent

---

[74] Leckie, *The Colonel's Lady on the Western Frontier: The Correspondence of Alice Kirk Grierson*. (University of Nebraska Press 1989).

him a communication on August 13, 1867, informing him as such, and on the 24th Graham sent his official acceptance of rank letter from Fort Hays to the Adjutant General.[75] On file with the National Archives is another acceptance letter from Graham, in his hand, erroneously dated August 18, 1868, not 1867 and reiterates that he was born in Crown Point, NY. He would soon alter that.

In the autumn of 1867 the headquarters of the 10th Cav was moved to Ft. Riley and more companies formed: troops I, K, L, and M. Each company was designated by the color of their horses[76] with Graham's Company I as "bay." It was organized on Aug 15 in time for his promotion.

Although HQ stayed at Riley for some time, Graham and his new company went west to guard the construction of the Union Pacific RR near Hays City. The route was to run to Denver along the Smoky Hill River. Previously known as Fort Fletcher, it had been recently renamed New Fort Hays when Graham arrived. Imagine movies or old TV Westerns, with stereotypical towns where shoot-ups took place frequently, dead bodies lying on dusty roads, or dirty looking townsfolk fighting over poker tables. Outlaws making their way into town, horses tied to posts with soiled doves weaving around, their tired eyes looking for men with a gold piece or two. Welcome to Hays City. Dangerous? Yes, and Hays was one of the worst. According to a diary written by Matt Clarkson in 1867, Hays had 22 saloons but one grocery store. A normal morning might involve at least one dead body on the streets.[77] One of the most commonly reported illnesses at Fort Hays at the time was venereal disease, along with diarrhea, flu, injuries, etc.

Fort Hays was even less comfortable. Only a few buildings existed in 1867-68, with many soldiers having not much more than a tent to protect them from the extreme summers and winters, and the rough, dusty winds. It was said that George A. Custer was angered that the hardtack sent to his men was actually made and boxed six years previous. It was a long way from the East Coast, and by the time any shipments arrived they were likely to be spoiled or bug-infested. Posts had cooks but these unskilled men had to make do with basics like beans, bread, and a mystery meal usually labeled "stew." Once in a while fresh buffalo meat would make a good meal, and as the train tracks were laid, towns sprang up, offering a bit more variety. Of course that variety was in the form of prostitutes, guns, booze...for Hays City had no church.

The soldiers at Fort Hays had calls every hour. Reveille, meals, fatigue, stable, retreat, there were these calls and more. On top of the living conditions, disease hit the fort during the first summer Graham was back in the Army. Cholera hit the city, with many citizens treated at the post along with soldiers. All of these situations resulted in high desertion rate. His wandering senses were probably bored senseless after serving in bustling areas.

Graham and his men weren't at their new job for long when a Company G soldier, which had two lieutenants in charge at that time, was attacked by 60-70 Cheyenne. Along with Pvt. John Randall were two civilian workers. The Indians killed the workers, scalped one, and severely wounded Randall with gunshot and lance-type

---

[75] Ibid.
[76] Company M would consist of remaining horses and named "mixed," but it was casually called "calico."
[77] *Old Fort Hays 1867-1889.* Hays Chamber of Commerce. 1959.

wounds. Randall was later found, half dead, hiding under a cut in a bank. He had killed several Indians before collapsing, hiding the entire time until help arrived. He survived the attack and witnesses heard the Indians comment on the fighting spirit of the black man who drove them off. Sgt. Davis, also of G, went after the attackers. A grisly sight was on the ground as Davis returned. A white man's scalp lie tossed on the ground. The Cheyenne compared him and the others to buffalo - "who had fought like a cornered buffalo; like buffalo they had suffered wound after wound, yet had not died; and who, like a buffalo had a thick and shaggy mane of hair."[78]

This, in autumn of 1867, was perhaps the first mention of the term Buffalo Soldier. Historians still debate as to its meaning, the consensus being that it referred to either the black soldiers' curly hair, their use of buffalo hide coats, and/or their fighting spirit. The coat theory is questionable at this early point in the origin as no one wore fur coats in August, but the large coats could have been additional description later. The date and area of this early mention leads one to wonder if the term Buffalo Soldier came not just from the 10th Cavalry indeed, but company G, who may have been commanded at the time of the incident by Graham if he was the senior officer in the area. Co. G had lieutenants in charge. It may be conjecture, but can anyone not be reminded of Graham's pride at being a Buffalo and leading Buffaloes in the Civil War? Graham and his band of looters took the insult and turned it into a backward compliment, even creating a song for themselves, the reader will recall. It is possible that Graham heard about the "enemy's" nickname for his men, despite it being complimentary, and used the term, harking back in his own mind to his former heroics. I doubt that Graham started the name Buffalo Soldiers for his men, but perhaps spread the new term in a boastful way, with the result that it kept the Indians' moniker from becoming something said in passing, otherwise forgotten. Was the proliferation of the term the result of a scoundrel's ego? The absolute truth may never be known. But as food for thought, let the readers digest the facts of name, time, and location and judge for themselves.

Out in the open prairies of Kansas another Buffalo was about to gain fame. William Cody was a scout for the 10th Cavalry at this time and tells of his experience with Graham. He recalled in his biography that he was hunting buffalo when some officers came out from the fort and wanted to join the hunt. Cody recognized their ranks as one captain and the others lieutenants. The officers did not know Cody. Graham asked Cody if he was on a hunt, then criticized Cody's horse. Cody played ignorant and asked Graham questions, pretending to be a beginner. Graham lectured Cody a bit on horses and tactics of hunting. Cody made a fool of Graham, shooting all the buffalo they came across and the officers not getting one shot in. Graham was very impressed and probably very embarrassed. Cody was enough of a good sport to give Graham and his officers some tongues and meat.

Like the moniker "Buffalo Soldier," it has been debated (at times very hotly among Wild West historians) that Buffalo Bill's nickname originated with that day with the 10th, with an argument ensuing over the name with Cody and William Comstock. Another possibility stems from a mention of Graham and "Buffalo Bill" in a newspaper article in November of 1867. That article made it widespread.[79] The most common thought is that

---

[78] Starr, "Buffalo Soldier," *Army Magazine*, January 1981
[79] Leavenworth *Daily Conservative*, Nov 26, 1867.

Cody "won" the name in a fight. This will no doubt be debated for many more years as well.

Other things were happening that would be lost to history or the details confused. While Maj. George A. Armes, the attractive, dark haired commander of Troop K, was still new in Hays City he arranged to have his meals in town at a hotel. Outraged at the number of gambling dens and brothels, he arranged for his brother Charles, who came to town in October, to solicit funds in Leavenworth to build a church in Hays. Armes, who bragged on himself and his morals at every opportunity, decided he would use the lumber for a dance hall/saloon once it reached Hays, with the transport furnished for free by the train who thought it was for a charitable purpose. The building was named the Globe Theater, later the Alhambra, and still later relocated to Fort Hays to become a gathering place for officers on post to have too much fun and drink. It is notable that in Armes's autobiography the entire church funding/dance hall saga is left out except for one mention of a new building. He does write that at that time he raised $400 to start a newspaper in Hays that didn't happen, so perhaps he later altered an embarrassing story. His later recollections left more than a few things out...

Around the same time, Armes was arrested by Capt. Samuel Ovenshine, the post commander, for fighting with another officer. He was in a courtroom with a lieutenant named Laufler, when the latter pulled a gun on Armes. Armes picked up a piece of wood and knocked the gun out of Laufler's hand, then reached out and twisted Laufler's nose in view of others. Armes, not Laufler was arrested, and later acquitted. He apparently spoke out and acted against anything he found offensive or took as a personal attack. He seemed to be on decent terms with Graham at first, for in October he had an enjoyable day watching other officers race horses, including Graham's lieutenant Myron Amick who had a fast horse, and at the end of the day he wrote that he and other officers had finished 87 bottles of wine at a party. But Armes, who would later boast that he had been court-martialed more than any other man in the service, was quickly becoming a thorn in the Army's side. Although he was brevetted for bravery with his 1867 Kansas battle, known as Prairie Dog Creek (and would claim that everyone was jealous of him), he spent more time nosing around and proffering charges against other officers than just about anything else. It didn't take him long to turn on Graham.

Hays itself was one of the wildest of Wild West towns. These were the years of Wild Bill Hickok, in a town where the shadiest of characters ran the streets and on any given morning the sun would rise on the bodies of those killed the previous night, still lying on the streets where they had been gunned down. Civilians had a different view of soldiers now that the Civil War was over. Many townsfolk thought soldiers hanging about town were no better than anyone else passing through looking for booze and trouble.

Whenever Graham was in Hays he apparently of time in the room of a fallen woman. This room may actually have been in Armes's Alhambra! He was gaining notoriety among soldiers and officers for having a "kept woman," repeating his habit from North Carolina, but this time she was a prostitute with her own place on the north side of town who went by the name Anne King. Whether his relationship with her was purely sexual or something else is unknown. He was accused by Armes of loading Annie onto his buggy and wildly riding around town, even bringing her onto post in full view of other officers. Later legends claimed that Graham was also getting used to nighttime carousing, often in civilian clothes, and making up for lost sleep during the day during those days before the bloody Indian battles in the area really started. These stories may or may not be true, as Graham would become sort of a scapegoat fodder for yellow newspapers after his death.

An incident did occur though at Annie's room. Sometime in the spring of 1868 Graham left his duties on Fort Hays, rode into town and, wearing his Officer of the Day sash, stormed into her house. Hearing voices in her room caused him to knock down the door. With fire in his eyes, he whipped out his saber and threatened the man who was in her bed. The man was later identified as Mr. Malcolm Graham, a scout for the 10th and no relation to the officer standing at the foot of the bed. Perhaps Graham was rounding up stray soldiers and scouts to get them back to the post. Or, was he looking for Josie?

During 1867, Josephine Jones Graham arrived in Kansas. In the state archives is a request from Graham to Col. Ovenshine, Post Commander, asking to leave Fort Hays for Fort Riley "to settle some private business" at the beginning of December. This may have been to meet up with her, as Riley was where anyone looking for the Tenth Cavalry would have traveled. Whether he gave her support or not is unknown, but she did have to work in a Hays hotel to take care of herself, so any support was "under the table." Men apparently still didn't know he was married.

Another curious incident at the end of 1867 may relate to his request for leave, especially if it did relate to Josephine's surprise trip to Kansas. On the 27th of December, Georgie received a rather stern request to explain his "conduct" in Hays City over the 24th and 25th of that same month. The conduct is not explained and his reply/excuse to Ovenshine is still unknown. A few ideas come to mind; perhaps Graham brought the Missus back to Hays, having little choice, and was angry or hell raising in town. Or, as Ovenshine was a few days from leaving Fort Hays, and Graham was to be placed temporarily in charge (!), he may have used that as an excuse to pull a stunt in town. That it was over Christmas Eve and Christmas Day may or may not have had anything to do with it.

One of the strangest items to fall into my hands is a copy of a letter from Annie King to her lawyer, Lucius Eaton, in St Louis. Dated June 10th, 1868, she tells her lawyer to write to her in Hays City *in care of* Mrs. G. W. Graham! So the wife and the alleged mistress were friends? Either Josie was the stupidest woman in town, or the accusations of him "keeping a prostitute" were exaggerated, and it was some other dealing he had with her. If Annie did live in Armes's saloon, she was likely filling Graham in with tidbits about the "morally superior" Armes. A man working at the Alhambra for Armes, William Goodale, later testified on Graham's behalf. More on that later. Getting back to Josie in Hays and Annie's astonishing relationship with her, Graham left for Leavenworth a week after Anie's letter of the 10th. We see by hotel arrivals listed in the Leavenworth *Daily Conservative* that George stayed at his Leavenworth "home," The Planters House. It could have been Army business or almost anything. Trying to get Josie out of Hays? With this boy it's hard to tell. Also listed as arriving at the same time from Fort Hays were a "Miss J. E. Ford" and a "C. B. Wilson" from Hays City. If they were traveling WITH him or just on their own is unknown. Did "J. E. Ford" secretly mean Josie?

Whatever he was doing though in Leavenworth doesn't seem to have been military related. Gen Sherman had given the OK for a road linking Hays and Fort Dodge, and it was reported that Graham was to be put in charge, and to be assisted by Jared

Sanderson, who was with the Southern Overland Mail Co. This was announced on April 1st. So Graham was likely somewhere between Hays and Dodge.

Whoever said that men don't gossip has never served in the Army. Armes, whose ear was always to the ground, had his own issues with the 10th Cavalry's chain of command by being in arrest frequently. He was getting fed up, as he later put it, watching Graham get away with his of behavior. Graham was also spending plenty of time gambling, both on and off post, and Armes was under arrest most of the time, accused of being disrespectful to his superiors by bringing flagrant misconduct to their attention. The arrests were, he claimed, revenge for reporting on the ill behavior of other officers. He was known as a brave officer and brilliant strategist, yes, but he was a pain in the neck as well, watching others like a hawk for any behavior he disliked.

Graham's card-playing partners likely included superiors, maybe even Col Benjamin Grierson.

According to a story in a Denver newspaper years after Graham's death, Wild Bill Hickok himself approached Graham in Hays City, after having had some argument previously. Hickok allegedly aimed a pistol at Graham who said he "wasn't fixed," meaning he was unarmed. Graham offered to fight Hickok outdoors with nothing but his bare hands, succeeding in giving him a good thrashing, and, it was claimed, the two became friends after that.[80] It's hard to imagine Graham unarmed, and the original source of this story hasn't been located. That issue also wrote about Graham having a personal fight with a train agent in town, resulting in both men having a shoot out with shotguns, Graham escaping injury and the agent taking shot to his leg.[81] Both are likely untrue, especially the Hickok tail. Hickok was in Hays, yes, but it was in 1869, when Graham was in Washington DC receiving a brevet.

George was a busy bee that spring of 1868. Besides gambling, scouting, Indian battles, and whatever was going on with two women, he was manipulating President Johnson's former secretary, Andrew Kennedy Long. How he became acquainted with Long is unknown, maybe through Long's job of heading commissary subsistence at the frontier forts, but Graham quickly ingratiated himself to the man. This would begin a total fabrication about his origins that would outlive him. In Graham's personal file at NARA, there is a letter from Maj. A. K. Long to Johnson, dated May 1868, and sent from Ft. Harker. In it, Long urged the President to make Graham a brevet lieutenant colonel for head-shaking reasons. Long pointed out that everyone else Graham served with had a brevet, so he should have one also. Long appealed to the President's roots by writing that Graham was a North Carolinian (like Johnson) and who went to New York at the outbreak of the Civil War to join a Union unit. Long summed up his reasoning by stating that Graham had been gallant in the War, emphasizing it by underlining "gallant," and added that Graham's previous service should earn him a brevet three years later, as if he was not commissioned for his past service in the first place.[82] Records show that the Senate rejected both a brevet major and a lieutenant colonel rank for Graham in July.[83]

---

[80] Denver *Daily Times*, Oct 27, 1877.
[81] Ibid. This is one of the rare post-mortem mentions of Graham's unknown adventures.
[82] Alexander K. Long committed suicide in 1878.
[83] Letters and their Enclosures Received by the Commission Branch of the Adjutant General's Office, 1863-70. M1064, National Archives, Washington DC.

It was at this time that Graham told another officer a very curious story about his origins. Col. Homer Wheeler wrote in his biography, *Thrilling Days in Army Life*, some recollections about Graham, who told Wheeler that he was originally from Charleston, SC, a graduate of something called the Charleston Cadet Corp,[84] and that he went north when the Civil War broke out. The book also claims that Graham boasted about being in prison in New York, and released upon the condition that he enter the service. Wheeler seemed to buy the contradictory stories. It is true that there was a common belief among the few who later drew on their memories of Graham that he had been in prison, probably in Clinton County, NY. No records exist from that pre-Civil War period. Rumors also persisted that Graham entered as a private and perhaps as a scout or spy, so impressed Gen. Grant that he singled out Graham, saying, "Make that man an officer!" Dramatic yes, but untrue. Graham's military files clearly show that he entered as a 2nd Lieutenant as a native of Essex County, NY. Wheeler's book is a fascinating read into the Frontier Army, but the stories had wrote about Graham are patently false.

Why though would Graham tell Wheeler that he was from *South* Carolina? It continued his pattern of alternating the truth with fiction, but telling a Vermonter that he was from the south is odd. If his father walked out on the family Graham may have been ashamed to admit this, as well as his hotel past, to superiors. Many of the men he ran with were West Pointers, others came from long, distinguished families. Though Graham had no reason to be ashamed of his family, he didn't want anyone knowing they were working-class either. As for the prison story, we may never know, but as Harriet Graham hinted later, her son had always been a handful and not averse to trouble. Graham may have told a few enlisted men about being in prison, maybe to intimidate, and somehow this morphed into the story that he was paroled to enter the service. Or it could simply be that Wheeler's memory wasn't so hot by the 1920s.

Another story in circulation at the time was that George had quite a bit of money after the Civil War, which jibes with reports of him playing the horses in New York. Wheeler claimed Graham earned plenty of kickbacks from enlisting blacks into Union service. His memory seemed fuzzy in his books, but Wheeler did recount various ways that Graham disciplined his men. When two of his soldiers fought, Graham equipped them with whips, making them fight it out until the men shook hands.

On another occasion a soldier took a gun and tried to shoot Graham, who, apparently pleased at the soldier's nerve, made the man an NCO. Graham also enjoyed using his men as Indian bait, putting them horseless in hollows of ground and waiting for Indians to appear so that he could ride up with all of the horses and shoot at the Indians.[85]

By autumn, Graham and his company had been relocated to Fort Wallace, KS. All was noisy on the western front by August 1868. Several companies went to protect workers building block houses on the Solomon and Saline Rivers. Indians had been tearing through the settlements and stealing livestock as well as attacking women. Those companies from the 10th Cavalry dispersed the Indians by mid-month.

---

[84] I have checked with the Citadel in SC and their historians have no knowledge or records of a Charleston Cadet Corps.
[85] Col. Wheeler, *Buffalo Days*, (Bison Books 1990).

Stage lines and work on the railroad meant more Indian attacks. Fort Wallace, near the Colorado border, was near what was known as Pond Creek at that time. It was a desolate post, the terrain scrub, and situated near what look like mesas you would see in New Mexico.

September and October were eventful and dangerous months. LtCol. Louis H. Carpenter and his Co. H engaged a terrible fight, known as the Battle of Beecher Island in September. Regardless of anyone's opinions of George or the Frontier Army, these were dangerous times in a dangerous area. Desertions could run high as men knew and saw what would happen to them if any Native Americans got hold of them.

Capt. Graham nearly lost his life along Beaver Creek, east of Hays, as he was ambushed and his horse's saddle came loose. The Indians had tried to cut him off from the rest of his comrades, and as Graham slipped from his horse, he grabbed its mane to hang on, eventually falling off as the horse galloped back to camp. Fortunately, his second, Lt Amick rode up and drove the Indians back.

There is evidence Graham was not with his company the entire month of September as he was listed in returns as arriving on post Sept 8 and went on sick leave, with Lt. Myron Amick taking charge of Co. I at least part of September.

Graham found himself in a terrible fight and was nearly killed again at the Battle of Big Sandy Creek. Not as well known as the Battle of Beecher Island, (and not to be confused with the infamous Sand Creek Massacre of 1864) it was documented in post returns as well as books and contemporary newspapers. The exact location is unknown and there are variances in the story, although early reports claim it was near the same spot as the earlier massacre. Books later written about it only mention it briefly, but do give some clues as to its location. Said to have been about twenty miles southwest of Cheyenne Wells, before Kit Carson City, along the Big Sandy. I went to that area on a freezing, windy day and the creek does run near an area where there are some slight hills perfect for ambushing soldiers.

Official military returns stated that Co. I, commanded by Graham, left Fort Wallace on the 5th for the Smoky River's north fork and returned two days later. After Graham arrived at Wallace they left again as a company to scout the Republican River and went back to the north fork of the Smoky to camp for the night. Col. Bankhead ordered a detachment from Co. I to scout the area west of the Cheyenne Wells area. This was likely Graham and a few of his men. They encamped on the Big Sandy and were attacked by 100 Indians with the fight running until dark. Returns go on to state that the Army lost ten horses. Large parties of Indians were in sight the entire night, and Graham and his detachment went back to Cheyenne Wells and on to Fort Wallace via Big Timbers. A slightly different version was found in an 1897 booklet, the *Roster of Non-Commissioned Officers of the 10th U.S. Cavalry*.[86] It reports that almost all of Co. I's horses were stolen, and that there may have been two waves of attacks, one just after dark while supper was being prepared when Indians rode through the camp knocking over everything, which in turn terrified the animals, beginning a stampede.

---

[86] Facsimiles were made from the original copy at Fort Davis NHS that belonged to 10th Cavalry veteran Capt. Robert Smither who joined the 10th in 1867.

They were not long back at Wallace before being ordered to assist in rescuing Sheridan's aide, Lt Col. Forsyth. The official returns report something notable: Lt. Amick was in command of Co. I at least part of the time during Forsyth's rescue.

Forsyth had been attacked by what was reported to be 700 Indians. Incredibly, a few of his scouts, including Malcolm Graham,[87] were able to get to Ft. Wallace for help. Carpenter took his company and Graham's, which consisted of 60 men to rescue Forsyth. Accompanying them were troops from the 5th Infantry and 2nd Cavalry. The rescuers found the poor wounded man in a hole, reading *Oliver Twist*, surrounded by decaying horses. His officers had been killed and no one had food save for rotting meat. He was very fortunate that his infected leg did not need to be amputated. [88]

Wheeler wrote about Graham at Big Sandy Creek. In his recollection, Graham, Amick, and Sgt. Burke chased after the Indians, and succeeded in recovering the horses. Also along, according to Wheeler, was the post surgeon, Dr. Turner. The doctor was very interested in the study of skulls for experiments in craniology and wanted to collect Indian skulls for the Smithsonian. After Sandy Creek, it was said that Burke delivered the three Indian heads in a bag to Turner at the latter's tent.

Less than one month later Carpenter with Co. H and Graham with Co. I, escorted Maj. Carr, 5th Cavalry, to Beaver Creek in Colorado Territory. After the party camped for the night in the area, Graham and two soldiers left at daybreak on a short scout to check the area for Indians as well as search for signs of previous trails left by the 5th Cavalry. Graham had not traveled far when some Indians came down over a hill and fired upon him. His saddle slipped and he had to hang onto the horse by its mane. Graham finally lost his grip and landed in a creek. The horse found its way back to camp, but Graham could only stand there and fire his weapon at the Indians. Lt. Amick rode up and ran the off the Indians. Why Amick was not breveted or recognized for his actions is unknown. *The Roster of the 10th Cavalry* claimed that Graham was out of ammunition and resorted to his saber by the time Amick arrived to save him. At this battle First Sgt. James Brown was noted by Carr to have suffered a bow attack that pinned both of his legs together.

On Nov 16 Graham and his men arrived back at Ft. Hays from duty on the terminus of the Union Pacific Rail Road.

Graham and Carpenter's companies left Fort Wallace again on Nov 21, 1868 to ride south toward the Arkansas River. Joining them was one company of the Thirty-Eighth Infantry, the entire expedition being under Carpenter's command.[89]

Returns say Graham and Carpenter, along with their lieutenants, were summoned to Fort Dodge in the spring of 1869. The lieutenants, Amick and Orleman of I and H respectively, were next sent to Camp Supply in Indian Territory for the summer to command the companies while Graham and Carpenter went to Washington. Recommended for brevets for their battles at Big Sandy Creek and Beecher Island necessitated their trip to Washington, DC to receive those brevets and take their oaths. Graham's name appears in the Leavenworth *Times*' list of prominent arrivals[90] in that city.

---

[87] Criqui, *Fifty Fearless Men*, (Walsworth Publishing 1993).
[88] Cheyenne Roman Nose was killed at the battle after having one of his spiritual practices violated. Because he had been served food with a metal implement he "knew" he would die that day.
[89] Rocky Mountain *News*, Nov 30, 1868.

The public read in that paper that he was staying at the Planter's Hotel on his way to Washington.

In March many brevet recommendations were put forth and were approved. Carpenter was breveted a full colonel, while Graham received a brevet Major, and signed the official oath on June 11, 1869. Those brevets were made retroactive to the conflicts.[91]

Despite being made a Major, there can be no doubt that Graham's blood boiled. His manipulation of Maj. Long failed, and repeated rejections that he be made a brevet Lieutenant Colonel were fresh in his mind. On top of it all, Louis Carpenter came from a long line of important men with roots and connections. Graham probably did not even know the whereabouts of his own father. It's no stretch to imagine him being courteous (or manipulative) of Carpenter, yet telling others while drunk that Carpenter received his brevet not from victory and heroics, but by connections. By the following year it would be apparent that there was no love lost between the two officers.

Back at Camp Supply, Amick and the other lieutenants encountered at least one Indian fight. The same day Graham was having his day in Washington, June 11, Camp Supply was surprised by a band of Comanche who attempted to stampede horses at Supply.

Capt. Charles G. Cox, 10th Cavalry, was arrested at Fort Harker while Graham was away. Armes had had him arrested once earlier, in April, for leaving post without permission. Armes had to bump it up to "close arrest" after Cox broke his original arrest and went off again being publicly drunk and rowdy. He was in trouble again in May for interfering with the scouts, but Armes granted him a temporary leave from being under a guard's watch. Cox had recently met the widow of a Capt. Scott and, to everyone's surprise Cox and the widow Scott were married that month with most of the post witnessing.[92]

Cox would not be long in arrest but hell was to break loose by the end of the year. Armes was up to his old self and proffered charges against Cox for drunkenness on duty, selling government property, and general conduct unbecoming an officer. Schofield wanted Armes punished for some personal reason, and had to let Armes go back to his post, not finding a kangaroo court to do his bidding according to Armes. Incredibly he had been accused of not bringing Cox's behavior to the attention of his superiors. Graham returned in August from a long celebratory leave feeling proud, and sat for his one known photograph, at the photography studio of E. E. Henry in Leavenworth, depicting a handsome man, looking to the right, wearing his new brevet rank on a slightly non-regulation uniform. Sadly, Brevet Major George had little time to wear his new rank; he was eventually charged. Armes's original complaint is here in its entirety.

> Colonel I have the honor to transmit herewith charges and specifications preferred against Bvt. Maj. G. W. Graham, Captain 10th Cavalry, and would respectfully request that he be brought to trial as soon as the General Commanding thinks it con-

---

[90] Leavenworth *Times*, April 15, 1869.
[91] The History and Legal Effect of Brevets of the Armies of Great Britain and the United States. Fry, James B. 1877. Courtesy of The Center of Military History, Carlisle Barracks, PA.
[92] Ups and Downs of an Army Officer. Armes, George A.

> venient. This man's reputation is so notoriously disreputable that no respectable lady can treat him with civility and courtesy due his uniform without incurring a taint upon her fair name, or, at least, to place her reputation in jeopardy. That the service should be purged of such characters is patent to all, as the respect which the uniform once commanded is rapidly diminishing, while the example which is shown by officers of this man's standing and reputation in associating with improper characters is highly damaging to the esprit dc corps of the Army. I have been told that his case has been brought up at Department Headquarters, but hushed up on the interference of Gen. B. H. Grierson, Colonel 10th Cavalry.
>
> Very respectfully, your obedient servant,
> GEO. A. ARMES,
> Capt. 10th Cav.,
> Bvt. Maj, U. S. A.

This started a back-and-forth of letters, with Armes's complaints brushed off. Armes was ridiculed for bringing charges against things that happened the previous year, as well as being accused of personal malice, but this time he refused to let up. Each response was more angry and revealing regarding Graham's behavior.

One such response from Armes included this paragraph:

> My experience in the service has given me an idea that when communications are sent through a subordinate officer to his superior that they cannot be returned to the writer "disapproved," but only for correction, if it need be. My desire is that the charges go forward without delay. Because an officer is a good gambler, a judge of intoxicating drinks, or a bully, it is therefore no reason why he should be shielded from the punishment his disgraceful acts so amply merit.

Armes also turned in a buddy of Grierson's, as well as the new Camp Supply commander, Col. Nelson. Nelson, Cox, and Graham drummed up charges against Armes for taking favors from visiting dignitaries. As if Armes's charges of visiting a brothel and gambling (nothing new among officers) Armes yelled that George had been harassing Armes's laundress, Sarah McGuire.[93] Of all women to proposition, it's unlikely he would chase after his enemy's laundress, or whatever she was. Later in his court-martial, this charge against Graham was dropped completely. Sarah McGuire was at the court-martial and apparently had no complaints against him.

In November Graham was arrested, not because of any vague charges, but something more serious: he was accused of stealing government property and reselling it, along with other charges that would not be made public. Graham liked horses so much he was now suspected of being the leader of a horse-thief gang. Grierson and his friends had

---

[93] Many prostitutes used the terms "laundress" or "washerwoman" to hide their true profession. However there is no evidence that Miss McGuire was a prostitute, as she was legally hired by Armes and spurned Graham's offers.

a dilemma. This was much more serious evidence against Graham than gambling and fighting. It looked like he and Cox were selling Army horses and Armes had the goods. Armes had transferred some of his papers, sans his diary, to Lt. Maxon, who took over Co. K. Maxon informed Armes of his likely takeover, being friends with Col. Nelson. Armes claims in his book that Graham "won the old imbecile over" with booze and gifts of government property.[94] Armes had few good words for many men in his later autobiography, calling many superior officers "old fools" and such.

On Nov 26, 1869, Special Order 213 directed Graham, Cox, and Armes to be transferred to Ft. Leavenworth to be held for a General Court Martial. Post returns show that they left on Dec 1. Two days later the private quarters of Maxon were mysteriously burned and destroyed. Nothing else was reported concerning the fire so one wonders if Graham didn't have someone torch the quarters of Armes's lieutenant out of revenge on the man who was responsible for his court-martial. Conveniently, Armes's personal papers were in Maxon's quarters and thus destroyed.

Another notable item is in the returns for the same month. On the 13th a correspondence came from Ft. Harker related to "certain horse thieves supposed to have left to Camp Supply, I.T." No names were given, at least in the report. Who were those horse thieves, and why were they not named but called "certain?"

On the way to Leavenworth, Graham's own horse, Red-stockings, had to be put down after being kicked by another horse, probably upsetting George greatly. He loved and valued that horse that had been with him for so long.

The Daily Kansas *Tribune* kept in touch with Graham, writing on the 11th of December an update on Indian affairs, in which Graham was quoted as saying, "There will be more trouble with the noble red man" to come the following spring, but Graham opined that they (the Indians) were quiet in winter as long as the government gave them clothing and food.

Though each man was technically in arrest awaiting a court-martial, they apparently had free run of the area. Armes made a visit to the city of Lawrence and in January he met Gen. Schofield's brother, a colonel, who appeared to be a "conspirator" along with Nelson in being very favorable to Graham.

Graham must have felt extremely confident in an acquittal. Anyone else would have been careful to keep his nose clean during this time but Graham was making quite a public nuisance of himself around Leavenworth City. While Armes enjoyed his time by socializing and writing letters to family and friends, Graham was "socializing" with the local police and judge. Armes also did something Graham didn't think necessary: he hired two good attorneys. Apparently a good amount of crookedness was dug up on Schofield, but was not revealed as to exactly what it was. Armes had to sell some of his property to pay the attorney fees, and a month after his arrest still had not been presented with the charges against him. By the middle of February Armes sent off a letter to Col. Sturgis of the 7th Cavalry asking that the wild Graham be placed in close arrest. A reply was sent to Armes. It refused, reading in part, "…placing a commissioned officer in close arrest is a step that I am very slow to take, and one that can only be justified in cases of an extremely rare character." The letter was written and signed on Feb 23 by Sturgis.

---

[94] Ibid.

Incredibly it did not stop Sturgis from placing Armes in close arrest, charged with "contempt" for writing that letter! By the time Schofield ordered the trial, the 7th Cavalry heard the story, with Gen. Custer himself wanting to intervene on Armes's behalf. Armes recalled in his book that Custer considered the charges against Armes "trumped-up."

Sturgis tightened his stranglehold on Armes by refusing the accused's request that he be allowed go back to his quarters to get his personal things, which were left unlocked. Armes was forbidden from speaking to anyone, which in Sturgis's mind meant that Armes simply couldn't have meals. Armes claimed to be on the verge of starvation before he was finally permitted to go to the mess under armed guard. Friends of Armes got word to him that the men sitting on the board were talking trash about him and that he had no chance of a fair trial.[95] Graham meanwhile enjoyed boarding in a room at the posh Planter's Hotel in town.[96]

Armes was eventually released. The Leavenworth *Times* reported on the 24th that they had erroneously reported that Graham had interceded on Armes's behalf. Graham did no such thing, as the *Times* "cheerfully" corrected.

The court-martial of Major George W. Graham began on April 6, 1870.

He would make entertaining press for the Leavenworth Times over the coming months. Despite currently being court-martialed, on May 29 the paper reported Graham arrested and fined $25 for assault and battery, upon who is unknown, but later we would read that an editor of a Leavenworth paper wrote some things about Graham that did not sit well with him, and that Georgie broke his famous gold-tipped walking stick over the man's head. The $25 fine may have been worth it. In June he was arrested and fined $45 for speeding around town in a wagon.[97] The next day they reported on an "interesting race" between a team of horses owned by Maj. Graham and another gray team from Lawrence, with Graham winning in two heats. Whether he thought his friends in high places would secure his freedom, or if he realized his career was over it debatable. A psychologist could have a fine case study on his behavior during his final months as an Army officer. Graham was now running publicly afoul of civil law.

Possibly his most serious crime that month was being arrested, along with a married woman, for "lewd and lascivious behavior." In those days that could have meant any number of things, but the woman in question, Andrewlina Collier, would appear in papers off and on in the coming years, becoming known as a con artist, enraging her neighbors with raucous parties, and getting arrested for illegally selling alcohol. Graham posted his $200 bail but left Collier in jail, charged with adultery. He may have left her there on purpose as she allegedly bilked a few hundred bucks from him.

Despite his familiarity with the local police, Col Grierson was still on his side. On June 6, Grierson sent a letter to Graham from Fort Sill. It hints that Graham sent a letter and copy of his defense to Grierson, and the colonel answered that he did not think that if the court were to find him guilty, it would not stand in Washington. Apparently Graham asked Grierson to intercede, and the man did, telling Graham he himself wrote to unknown contacts in Washington, testifying to Graham's worth as an officer and standing

---

[95] Ibid.
[96] Leavenworth City Directory. 1870-71.
[97] Leavenworth *Times*, June 9, 1870.

by his character.

There was also some wild story which circulated, AFTER his death of course, which claimed that he was running with some prominent citizen's daughter, got himself engaged to her, and was "hauled off in chains" under arrest (for his charges) the night before the wedding was to have taken place. Another version is that Graham was ordered to Fort Hays or Fort Riley to KEEP him away from this woman. Hard to believe but there was a story in one Kansas paper that Georgie was driving wildly through Leavenworth streets with a blonde actress who had a pushy stage-mother, trying to make her spoiled girl a stage star despite the girl's zero talent. If this is true, there was a young actress named Lucia Sinclair. She was in her early twenties, from Wisconsin, and died in 1875 from consumption. Not much else is known but her living arrangements in Leavenworth fit that description. Another one for the "Mystery File" in my cabinet.

COURT-MARTIAL[98]

The charges (abbreviated) against Bvt Maj. George W Graham were:

CHARGE 1 - Conduct Unbecoming an Officer and a Gentleman

Spec 1 – Took a notorious prostitute riding through the camp of Fort Hays, KS.
Spec 2 – Attempted to sell to Lt. Maxon a government branded horse at Camp Supply, I.T.

A specification later dropped for no known reason was that he neglected and disowned his legal wife, Josephine Graham, necessitating her work at a hotel in Hays City to support herself while he kept a prostitute, Annie King, with the resulting scandal of the service from approx. February through June in Hays City. Another one, also dropped, was that he harassed Sarah McGuire, a laundress, and attempted repeatedly to get her to his tent for prostitution.

CHARGE 2 – Wrongfully and Knowingly Selling or Disposing of Government Property

Spec 1 – That he sold to Lt. Badger one bay horse, government branded.
Spec 2 – That he bartered or conveyed a chestnut sorrel horse to Lt. Banzhaf a horse furnished to be used in the US military.
Spec 3 – Did knowingly sell one roan horse branded government property to Lt. Amick.
Spec 4 – Did knowingly sell one bay horse branded government property to Col Crosby.

---

[98] RG 153: Records of the Judge Advocate General's Office (Army) Entry 15: Court-Martial Case File PP-1227, National Archives, Washington DC.

CHARGE 3 – Conduct to the Prejudice of Good Order and Military Discipline

Spec 1- He did visit a house of prostitution in the uniform of Officer of the Day and raise a disturbance with Malcolm Graham.

Horse stealing. Lewd behavior and assault. Harassing women. Hauling prostitutes to Ft. Hays. What was real and what was in Armes's mind? Was Georgie really stupid enough to harass Armes's laundress, of all people? Maybe she was a laundress in another sense of the vernacular to Armes himself. But George was married, and the poor, determined wife made her way from New York to Kansas, hoping to win his love back or at least be near him.

If any other officer or soldier knew about his marriage they kept it mum. Josephine Graham only turns up in the court-martial transcripts and a later newspaper article. More surprisingly this charge was dropped in the trial. She was listed as a witness from New York, but the charge was not written up in detail and crossed out like the Sarah McGuire incident. A charge drawn up and then *ignored*. Maybe Josephine felt sorry for him and asked that there be no charges, but the reason for this missing information is not apparent. The only thing known from research up to this point in his life is that she was wed to Graham in 1865, and later followed him to Hays where he refused anything to do with her, giving her no choice but to take a job at a hotel. As for the McGuire incident, it is marked through with a large X in the documents.

The most incriminating testimony regarding Annie King came from Lt. Charles F Banzhaf. It was noted by a few observers that, when King rode into Fort Hays with Graham, she motioned to Banzhaf by nodding and lifting her veil. Another bit of information was about to break. There was a reason she greeted Banzhaf: he had known her husband from the Civil War!

While Graham denied that the woman in his buggy was a "notorious prostitute," and a few admitted that they were unsure who she was, other men were certain it was King, a few admitting that they were familiar with her house of ill repute. As Graham, basically defending himself while his counsel watched, kept objecting, Banzhaf stated under oath that he recognized her as Annie King, or as he knew her years ago, Mrs. Barr. Graham's aim in objecting was that, if he did not know she was a prostitute, he couldn't be guilty of conduct unbecoming an officer. The court was cleared and when resumed, Graham was overruled. Banzhaf told how he had been friends with the disreputable woman's husband and knew her from years earlier in Missouri as Anna Barr. She was the widow of Capt. William Barr of the 2nd Missouri Cavalry, aka Millett's Horse. William died at the end of 1874 at a Denver post hospital due to illness contracted at Vicksburg and Anna Barr was granted $20 per month pension. Apparently she had developed an affinity for Army men, moved east and, it was claimed in court, never sent "anyone with a greenback away unsatisfied."[99] She was also referred to as a tasty little morsel in the court-martial papers! Oh, to have been a fly on that wall..

---

[99] Annie King was born Anna Johnson in Texas. I have only found the name of one sister, Celia Pierson. It is not known why she took the name "King."

The hero of Beecher Island, Louis H. Carpenter, testified for the prosecution that he did see the woman in the buggy nod toward Banzhaf although Carpenter did not know who she was. Since Banzhaf served with Barr's husband and no doubt knew her, the fact that he identified the woman in the buggy as Anna Barr was damning.

Other officers told how it was common knowledge that King was a "woman of the town." They all told of her house on the NW side of Hays City. Annie unintentionally wound up the subject of laughs in the courtroom when a letter from her was read, a letter notarized no less, that said she was in Kit Carson city when the buggy ride occurred. Most of the officers felt it ridiculous to take the word of a "whore."

In his defense, the testimonies that George was riding around with Annie were divided. About half of the witnesses/officers say it WAS Annie, others say it was not, and may have been the wife of a local man named Moses. He also called the other men out, saying that just because a woman may be a prostitute does not mean she should be laughed at.

Graham's rebuttal to the charges is a fascinating study into his speech and way of thinking, not to mention brazen arrogance. He actually had booklets printed containing the rebuttal. How many he had made will never be known. The only one I have seen lies in his court-martial file at NARA. A portion is reprinted here to illustrate his attitude. The entire spiel is at the end of this book for posterity.

> "...Malice overreached itself and only evinces its disposition to wrong me by the preference of the charges which it was impotent to establish. The elegant and accomplished Maj. Armes, to whose regard for the public service I am indebted for my appearance here, was not present to confront me, but the Judge Advocate has perhaps exercised as much skill in restraining him from mounting the witness stand with his black book, as he has in confining others of his trusty witnesses in the guard house for the acknowledged fear that their sturdy Spartan virtue might be tampered with."

Graham, while defending himself, seems to throw insults to the judge. It is interesting to note that Armes, his accuser, was not at the court-martial and was not brought in to testify.

At the same time Graham was both being court-martialed and getting arrested in Leavenworth, "important information" was on its way to Washington from his lawyers, info that was claimed to be urgent and the attorneys asked for a final decision to wait until that info be examined. Unfortunately, all that exists of whatever it was is an empty envelope in the court-martial file at NARA and a copy of a telegram in his military file. It could possibly have been another stall, just like the one back in New Bern where an important witness, Capt. Jocknick, was brought in for nothing. Also missing is Exhibit A. It is possible that Exhibit A was Graham's scrapbook of the recommendations that enabled him to get a commission in 1866. Copies are on microfilm at NARA.[100]

In August Graham was found guilty on some counts of the 1st and 3rd charges, and one of the four specifications of the 2nd. Guilty of selling one horse that even his own lieutenant testified that Graham had won in a race in his presence, and the charge of

---

[100] Graham had this scrapbook of newspaper clipping and praise from fellow officers in his possession at least one year before his death. What happened to it is unknown.

riding around Hays with Annie King. Not exactly the crime of the century, but his career was over.

A life ended. Chances, as far as Kansas went, were used up.

Graham was publicly humiliated on that last day at Fort Leavenworth. His cashiering likely took place on the grounds around Sumner Place, with troops witnessing superiors removing his rank, taking his sword, and dismissing him from post, no longer a fancily dressed officer but a disgraced, jobless civilian. That humiliation probably damaged his psyche in many ways. He had been an Army officer since age 23. He had been honorably discharged from a bloody war, returning home a hero. Now he was left with nothing. One can imagine that mustachioed face on his tall body, leaving Fort Leavenworth as a plain citizen. Knowing him like I do, I doubt he looked shamed. He probably held his head high, showing no emotion, but burning with anger inside. Who knows what the other officers thought, though if Armes had been there, he was probably grinning. I doubt he showed up unless absolutely ordered. After all, he proffered the court-martial charges, yet didn't show up at the trial. Graham's soldiers, what did they think? For the most part they respected him, and he had no desertion rate to speak of.

On Sept 8, The Leavenworth *Times* reported it all to the little town's readers. His court-martial papers were sent to Townsend for forwarding to President Grant. He was sentenced to be cashiered, fined $500, would serve two years in prison, or more if the fine could not be paid, and immediately ceased to be an officer in the United States Army. Furthermore, it was forbidden for any officer to associate with him. Graham did get out of the prison sentence upon request of General of the Army, William T. Sherman. Whether Sherman knew Graham from news items, remembered him from an undiscovered message clear back in March of 1865, or through the influence of a counsel is unknown.

The *Philadelphia Evening Telegraph* reported in November that Graham's cashiering left "a desirable vacancy."[101] When the Frontier Army wasn't fighting Indians, they were fighting each other. Armes had his way, getting his nemesis booted out, but he was also out, via his own court-martial. Yet Armes had a long family tree and money from investments in real estate. The announcement of George's cashiering made several national newspapers, including the New York Herald. His family probably found out this way. By the time his family heard the news via the papers, Graham had moved on. Letters sent to Kansas went undeliverable. His mother was worried and desperate to find him.

Col. Wheeler wrote that Graham probably wasn't destitute at the time of his cashiering. Wheeler reported that Graham had at one time $4000 in the company safe. Was it another rumor, or did he save his pay, or bring money left over from the Civil War?

It was time to start another life, but, for the first time since he was a young man, he had no ideas, nothing to look forward to, no big plans. Or maybe he did. For some reason he didn't return to New York this time. He went further west, and he went without Josie. She became pregnant that same month but gave birth nine months later somewhere in New York. One can imagine Georgie telling her he would finish Army things, or clean up this or that, and return to New York. So off she went on that long train ride back to New York, probably not knowing she was pregnant.

Whether George was guilty of every horrible accusation or the victim of Armes's

---

[101] November 2, 1870.

slightly psychotic troublemaking is unknown. Indeed, Graham himself would later tell a journalist, from his cell in a Denver jail, that his court-martial was "just politics." One wonders if Armes simply hated Graham so much that he made himself a squeaky wheel until he succeeded in getting his enemy kicked out. Those later recollections by Armes? The Man of Morals who took charity money to build a saloon/dance hall had a pretty salty tongue, as alleged by other sources. The Globe/Alhambra that he owned? Annie King may have lived in one of the upper rooms! Armes's hired civilian saloonkeeper, William Goodale, testified ON Graham's behalf at the court-martial. When Goodale later recollected something he felt was important, he went to Lewis Merrill, the Judge Advocate, to officially do the right thing and make a slight change. Merrill basically told him to pound sand. Oh, and Lewis Merrill himself was just a few years later found to have been taking cash for securing acquittals/prosecutions!

      Did George W. Graham, Company I's first commander, suffer at the hands of "politics" as he later claimed?

Utah Nellie

Salt Lake City in 1870 was still developing. The famous Temple had been started nearly twenty years before and was still under construction. The railroad had just been connected via Promontory Point. That development was the catalyst for change, and where religion was almost inseparable from nonreligious activities, the town was not as isolated and others came to mine or set up businesses.

Graham's next life began here at the end of 1870. Why he seems to have made a beeline to Salt Lake City is a mystery. He used the title "Major" as though he hadn't just been stripped of it. Did he have ideas on setting himself up as a big shot in the burgeoning government, or try to take advantage of those Mormons he'd heard about? I suspect, and the reader can draw conclusions, that George was just about destroyed. He had been an officer since age 22, and now as a man of only 31, his career was gone. He may have always been on the edge of trouble, and was thinking he now hadn't much to lose.

Predictably it wasn't long before he made himself known as such a lowlife that some of the worst people in town didn't want anything to do with him. He was making a nuisance of himself in gambling dens and illegally making money as a "check-ranger," writing out phony checks on one bank to cash at other banks. It was one thing to be a con artist, but by this time Graham may have lacked the style that was seen in successful saloonkeepers, gamblers, and other rakes.

Despite this, his good looks and ability to speak well attracted the eye of at least one young Mormon woman who wasn't what she first seemed to be when she stormed into the offices of Justice of the Peace Alderman Jeter Clinton on March 22, 1871, and filed a complaint against George W. Graham.

Twenty-year old Ellen "Nellie" Adams[102] claimed he did, on or about Jan 1, take her to an inn at a hot spring, get her drunk on elder wine, and attempted an assault upon her. Miss Adams stated in that report that Graham again repeated his assault, soiling her, around eight days later. Immediately a warrant was issued for Graham's arrest. He was quickly found and hauled in to appear before Justice Clinton. Graham asked for and was granted a one-day extension before the hearing. The next morning witnesses were sworn in by the prosecution, and Graham asked for another delay of the hearing to gather his own witnesses. This request was also granted. Meeting at 10am on March 24, the evidence presented to both sides convinced Clinton that Graham was probably guilty. Clinton ordered that Graham be officially tried on the charges at the Third Judicial District Court at the next available session. On that day the Salt Lake *Herald* stated that the details were "too disgraceful for publication." A letter in the Utah Archives[103] dated April 4

---

[102] Listed as Nellie in the police records. Ellen did go by Nellie on occasion in later years.
[103] Official Transcripts and Marshal/Justice Correspondence on Arrest in Utah Territory Courtesy of: *Third District Court (Salt Lake County), Case Files, People vs Graham, Utah State Archives and Records Service, Series 9802*

by Justice Clinton orders M. T. Patrick, U.S. Marshal for the Utah Territory, to hold Graham on $2000 bond.[104]

If this all wasn't juicy enough for the local wags, imagine the gossip when The Deseret News reported that the girl's stepfather, Joseph P. Risley, showed up with a gun at the courthouse and fired two shots at Graham as they were hauling him away. "Graham's Luck" was in full effect: both shots missed. He screamed expletives at Risley in the street as a second officer dragged the man away. Risley was soon ordered to post $2000 bond, but, unlike Graham, he had plenty of friends who piled into the courtroom, eager to pool their money together to free the man who'd attempted to avenge his daughter's shame.

Meanwhile Graham's lawyer found some error in the mittimus ordering the jailer to hold him, a writ of habeas corpus was issued and, in true Graham-style, he sent off an angry letter on the 7th of April to Judge James B. McKean, notorious for his anti-Mormon sentiments and his harassment of Brigham Young. The letter protested that Marshal Patrick, who merely had a warrant for Graham's arrest and nothing more, was holding Graham illegally. He ended the letter by demanding that he be discharged from imprisonment. Judge McKean agreed that there was indeed an error and reduced Graham's case to a lesser court. The Deseret News was not favorable to Graham; always placing his title "Major" in quotes and sarcastically referring to him as an estimable member of society. On the other hand, the same journalist was pleased that a U.S. Marshal admitted a mistake and rectified it, perhaps setting a precedent in the Utah Territory. Bail was supposedly set at $2000, but on April 19 in the presence of Marshal Patrick, Graham posted a lessened $1000 bail acknowledging him and three other men indebted for that amount. The Deseret News asked why, if the bail was set at $2000, did Graham only have to post $1000, and wasn't a mere $1000 punishment for rape an insult to the claimed morality of the area? This very same article must have been rushed to press, as it ends with an additional bit: Facts had come to light which in part exonerated the public official and promised to update the reader in the next week.[105] The Deseret News apparently had found quite a story, but the whole thing disappeared from the public newspapers, maybe because it was not at all favorable to Nellie.[106]

The three men putting up the funds for Graham's release were H.C. Lincoln, P. Bartlett, and K. Smythe. The original handwritten contract is remarkable. Where the mention of the accusation of rape is in the complaint, Nellie Adams's name is written but then marked through though it can still be read. Graham's name and the names of his bondsmen have the same odd treatment, signed but marked through later. Also in this bail contract, obviously written ahead of time, the month and date of when Graham was to have appeared before the Third Judicial District Newspapers was left blank!

Graham walked out of confinement with a promise to appear in court on no particular day whatsoever. The paper simply went to "The Territory of Utah, County of Salt Lake." Newspapers had a field day questioning the actions of lowering bond to almost

---

[104] Ibid.

[105] The Deseret News (Utah), April 19,1871.

[106] Ellen H. Adams was born in PA in Oct 1849 to John and Hannah McMinn Adams. After John's death Hannah and her mother Mary moved from PA to UT in 1860 as part of the First Perpetual Emigrating Fund Co. Hannah married James P. Risley, from Salem NJ.

guarantee the escape of a criminal, which is most likely what happened. It also came to light that the bondsmen, Smythe, Lincoln, and Bartlett, had attempted to post bail at the Justice's Court but were refused on the grounds that they did "not appear competent" so they took their $1000 to the District Court where it was accepted. Naturally, Graham fled the Utah Territory afterwards. Were the shady bondsmen in cahoots with Graham, or did he stiff them, or was that $1000 a bribe put in McKean's pocket?

Regarding Judge James B. McKean, Civil War buffs may know that he was a colonel with the 77th New York Regiment, one arm of it being recruited in Saratoga Springs no less. Could Graham have met McKean if they'd both been in Saratoga Springs after the war? Or did Graham, always having his packet of recommendations and accolades handy, have "talked shop" with McKean, painting himself as just a fellow New Yorker and Civil War officer, in trouble with a local Mormon family? Remember, one of his recommendations in his packet was from Gen U. S. Grant, the same man who appointed McKean to his post. Bribing McKean, or depicting himself as a former Union officer with glowing heroics, victimized by a Mormon, would not be out of the question for Graham's character. When he was desperate, there was no such thing as sinking too low.

As always, there is far more to the story. What the local paper discovered earlier was this: Miss Adams had been seen in the company of Graham "all winter"[107] and the idea of a rape taking place outdoors in the dead of cold was questioned, as was why ten weeks had passed since the first assault before Nellie reported it. Also in those court documents was the admission that Nellie and Graham both admitted to cohabitation. It wasn't a "rape at an old mill" as had been claimed. But what doubtless local tongues wagging was the part that Nellie was seen at a pharmacist's buying "questionable" drugs.[108] In 19th century lingo this could have meant several things. Was she was seeking birth control, or worse, was she buying something to induce an abortion?[109]

Why the sudden disappearance of any news (until November) relating to Graham and his escape? McKean was being accused of anti-Mormonism at the same time, and one would think newshounds would have jumped on the fact that McKean lowered the bail on a non-Mormon from back East who may have attacked a Mormon girl. Reporters had proof that Nellie had been "soiled" before January, and if McKean did help Graham escape, it would inadvertently be helping the "victim" as well, for the woman had not been attacked at all. We can also question why Risley, her stepfather, took a couple of shots at Graham if they had been living together, unless "cohabitation" in that sense meant dating. About six months after he fled, Graham became a father. On Oct 4, 1871 Nellie gave birth to a girl whom she named Belle (Bella in some censuses). After Ellen "Nellie" Adams married a saddler four years later, (a very notable time as the reader will learn) the girl would become Belle Adams Mower.

To sum up the "Utah Nellie" affair, both she and Graham admitted in court that they had been living together for what looks like roughly December 1870 through March 1871. Suddenly she reported him for a rape occurring a few months prior, and after she

---

[107] Rocky Mountain *News*, June 12, 1874.
[108] Ibid
[109] Abortion drugs for women were hardly effective but dangerous. Concoctions were billed with warnings that taking it could kill an fetus but that warning was usually a disguised ad for abortion.

was spotted buying "suspicious" drugs at a chemist's. The birth record for Belle is missing but her death certificate gives proof that Graham was the father in the form of Belle's birthday, as she was born nine months after the alleged "rape."[110] It was not uncommon for a woman in trouble claim rape to save her reputation.

In November of 1871 the Salt Lake *Herald* ran an article mentioning a letter Harriet Graham mailed to unknown authorities in Salt Lake City from Crown Point.[111] Somehow she had word that he was in Utah and tried to find him. That letter asked that, if anyone knew his whereabouts, would they contact her through her local post office. Harriet obviously did not know that she was now a grandmother to a one-month old baby.

This so-far undiscovered letter, not reprinted but paraphrased, tells how Harriet was worried about her son and that his life of trouble was nothing new to her, how he'd always been a problem. This same article, running on Nov. 11, some seven months after Graham's jump, finally asks the questions the Deseret *News* promised to look into. The Salt Lake *Herald* claimed that the public wanted more info on the case and questions his release, and almost guaranteed escape by a court that prided itself on high moral standards. The paper also wanted to know why Graham's bondsmen had not been gathered up and questioned. No answer was ever given.

Poor Harriet. Graham was breaking his mother's heart. From all of the research it seems likely she never saw her Wallace again, although they were likely in correspondence after this.[112] She probably never knew of her granddaughter. Wallace would find himself the subject of news again, which Harriet would read about. His luck would be used so frequently it was only a matter of time before it would burn itself out.

Weren't the Utah authorities aware that "Capt. Graham" was making news in Leavenworth again? The newspaper of that city, the *Times*, reported on July 23 that Graham was arrested for larceny of a horse. Instead of fleeing to another territory immediately, he went back to Leavenworth. He may have had a few friends left in that city. On the 27th a writ of habeas corpus was applied for in his name, reasons unstated, again reported in the Leavenworth *Times*. The Utah papers had fun for awhile, writing about Graham's skill at the faro tables, his knack for helping out the underdog in situations, and that he usually had a few jealous women around ready to fight over him.

It would have been easier if he had gone home to Mother in New York, or Josephine, wherever she was. Instead he went west.

---

[110] California Death Index, 1940-1997, *FamilySearch* (https://familysearch.org/ark:/61903/1:1:VPW5-NB2 : accessed 13 April 2015), Belle Benbrook, 22 Jun 1960; Department of Public Health Services, Sacramento.
[111] The date and exact content of Harriet's letter is unknown.
[112] The letter from his mother refers to his name as "G. Wallace Graham." Matching the Wallace Graham in the New York census, it appears she preferred to call him Wallace.

It is hardly worth while to relate that Graham is in jail for seduction. Every one familiar with Graham's weakness will suspect it at once, but it may perhaps be interesting for readers to know that the victim is a Mormon girl. Doubtless the Graham strut on the pave and the roll of the Graham fine eye lured the unsuspecting Mormon beauty into the snares of destruction. It is the same old story; and you ladies who read it around your breakfast table think no more of it. It was Graham's way, but Brigham was too much for him.

Excerpt from article in the Leavenworth Times, April 12, 1871

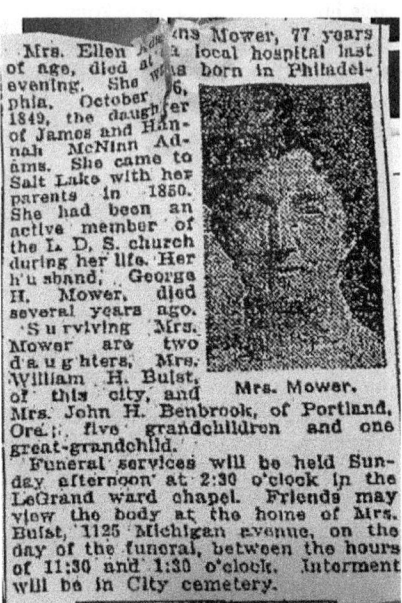

Mrs. Ellen Adams Mower, 77 years of age, died at a local hospital last evening. She was born in Philadelphia, October 6, 1849, the daughter of James and Hannah McNinn Adams. She came to Salt Lake with her parents in 1850. She had been an active member of the L. D. S. church during her life. Her husband, George H. Mower, died several years ago. Surviving Mrs. Mower are two daughters, Mrs. William H. Buist, of this city, and Mrs. John H. Benbrook, of Portland, Ore.; five grandchildren and one great-grandchild.

Funeral services will be held Sunday afternoon at 2:30 o'clock in the LeGrand ward chapel. Friends may view the body at the home of Mrs. Buist, 1125 Michigan avenue, on the day of the funeral, between the hours of 11:30 and 1:30 o'clock. Interment will be in City cemetery.

Mrs. Mower.

This low quality clipping is the only photo I have found of Ellen Nellie Adams

Last Chance, Colorado

What Graham did for most of 1872 is a mystery, although during the winter he tried to organize a mining expedition by advertising in newspapers. One such ad he placed in the Rocky Mountain News[113] reads:

Ho! For Arizona!

{Any one having $100, wishing to join a party going to Arizona for mining purposes, can obtain full particulars on applying to Maj. G. W. Graham, over Willoughby's shop, corner of Larimer and K streets, on Thursday evening next at 7 o'clock.}

In addition to Graham, two other men are mentioned as being organizers of this expedition. J. W. Read was a foreman with Billings and Moffat, at that time on Lawrence Street, a company that made doors, blinds, etc. Charles Hilliker, a carpenter with that company, was the other.[114] As for their meeting location, Willoughby's was another carpentry shop. A similar ad gives a different location for a general meeting: his own residence, a boarding house at 373 Larimer.[115] (The Denver directory lists his home as a boarding house on the west side of E Street, between Larimer and Lawrence). Another ad ran in May, this time with Graham saying he is a recruiter and fully competent to take this type of group into the land of the Apaches. It would be organized under military rules with squads having their own outfits and men will furnish their own revolvers and breech-loaders, and limited bags to fifty pounds each.

One supposes by this time in his life he only knew how to organize men who would take military style orders. Graham could easily have obtained a job in Denver, but one wonders if he wasn't hoping to command another group of looters to explore the Southwest. Graham had no intention of going straight, or at least hold down a proper job without being the commander.

The men, if they did succeed in organizing and going to Arizona, must have been unsuccessful. Perhaps they were not skilled in that area or the whole thing was a ruse to take interested parties' money and run.

His whereabouts after spring of 1872 and into 1873 are unknown. He may have even reconnected with Annie King, who was probably in the Kit Carson City area. After his death, the *Colorado Springs Gazette* reported that during his Colorado life he "deteriorated into an idler, gambler and desperado during a year's sojourn around here." He was eventually back in Denver, making that city his base of operations, and was a pest in the area hanging around saloons, gambling, and generally being a low-life.

---

[113] Jan 18, 1872.
[114] Hilliker, according to census, was in 1880 a prospector living in Silver Cliff, very close to Rosita.
[115] A year later in the 1873 Denver directory Graham is listed as boarding on E Street between Larimer and Lawrence.

Denver City certainly had its share of hoodlums. The whole of the Colorado Territory and anywhere its rail lines ran brought not only homesteaders and businessmen, but also ne'er-do-wells, prostitutes, and outlaws. The newly built Colorado Territorial Prison was already holding many criminals. For example, in May of 1871, George Witherell, convicted of taking an axe to a sheepherder, attempted to bash the head of a guard and escape. Previously, he had made a copy of a key out of soap and removed his irons.[116] Witherell was just one of many good-for-nothings who needed constant watch.

Graham had one mention in the Rocky Mountain News in May of 1873 that actually had nothing to do with a crime. A group of nineteen citizens volunteered to be scouts to fight Indians, sending a letter to Gen. Sherman, their names attached, and even mentioning the following as references: Wild Bill Hickok, Gen. Palmer, some other officers, and Majors Graham and Brooks. This item is very interesting. If Major Brooks was a Paymaster, it's a startling coincidence, as later that same year Brooks and Graham would cross paths in a way that would guarantee him never wanting to be on the same type of list as Graham. Of course Graham was not a Major anymore so the author either didn't know about Graham's dismissal or did not care. A former captain, Samuel Roberts, signed the letter to Sherman. The paper merely stated that it was "handed us for publication." By whom? The same Samuel Roberts, in another account, offered sixty local men for service, if the government would only supply their weapons, horses and food. Was Graham one of the locals? No records have yet been found for a Samuel Roberts, captain, formerly of the U.S. Army during 1866-72. It's safe to assume however that Graham was one of the men who volunteered, maybe while sitting around in a saloon with other former Army soldiers and discussing the "Modoc problem in California" and how they would handle it. Attaching Graham's name to a letter to W.T. Sherman may have been a mistake, had Sherman had any interest in this idea. Sherman signed off on Graham's court-martial less than two years prior. Graham should have known this, and Roberts, the letter writer, probably had no clue that Graham's contact with Sherman was via court-martial, and perhaps not by the cavalry hero's personal delivery of a message to Sherman during the last days of the war. One imagines Graham told that story repeatedly to anyone around, whether it was an officer, the town floozy, or a bored drunk in a den. He certainly made friends with the ne'er-do-wells of Denver as well as at least one woman. These "friends" were questionable at best. Stories would circulate about Graham's friendless-ness, that he was so strong and athletic that many men feared him. An unnamed Pennsylvania physician visited him after his next "act," and declared him to be almost unique in his perfect physical symmetry.

By autumn of 1873 Major Graham decided he would make his fortune by old-fashioned robbery. It was later said that he had been going around Denver announcing that he "would soon be heard from" and that he had a saying: "I am one of the boys that fears no noise, nor anything, nor anybody that draws breath."

The 6th U.S. Cavalry was now stationed at Fort Wallace to prevent attacks from Indians along the UPRR routes. One imagines the soldiers never thought danger would come from a former Army officer. Graham knew the route well and after his court-martial it

---

[116] Canon City *Times*, May 1, 1873.

appears he returned to some of these western forts in Kansas when he needed a place to stay despite the orders of his sentence that no Army person associate with him.

At daybreak on Sept 10, 1873 an ambulance from Fort Wallace, KS was making its way to the camp of the 6th U.S. Cavalry near River Bend, Colorado Territory. Cavalry paymaster Maj. Brooks, the post trader's wife (Mrs. Roberts), and a few soldiers met up with two officers from the 6th U.S. Cavalry, Capt. John A. Irwin and 1st Lt. William Wetmore.

Brooks was delivering pay to those stationed in the nearby camp. Suddenly the stillness was disturbed when shots rang out as two masked bandits rode up and demanded the money on board. Wetmore, fresh from West Point, used his pistol to shoot one of the highwaymen. After the dust settled, Irwin was wounded with buckshot to his back, Brooks took a shot to his lap, and Mrs. Roberts was also shot in her wrist.

As for the wounded robber, the ball from Wetmore entered near his heart and left quite a hole in his back. When he was unmasked the officers were aghast. They recognized the face. Another quirk: Graham lay on the ground dying near Big Sand Creek, the same creek where he had earned his brevet. Was it possible in his arrogant mind that robbing a cavalry paymaster would be revenge upon the Army for not getting the brevet he wanted and being cashiered?

His partner-in-crime, John Dyck, fled and locals would guess that he made his way to the border as he was not seen again despite a manhunt which stopped where Dyck's tracks did: Hugo, a spot on the map east of Denver.[117]

The victims were treated and returned to Fort Wallace. The search was on for accomplice John Dyck. No certain mention was found of him other than that some unverified sightings around town and at a blacksmith's. The whole incident was quickly reported in newspapers across the country, each one making sure to include the juicy bit that one of the bandits was a former officer with the 10th U.S. Cavalry.

Graham himself was hauled off to a Denver sick room in a building adjacent to the actual hospital, partially because there was no room in the city jail. He was so mortally wounded he was not expected to live. It was noted that he had a wound that looked like he had been pistol whipped to the forehead. Since he was found face down, did someone turn him over as he was down and crack him in the face? Obituaries sprang up in papers. It was not unusual for these obits to mention Graham as despicable. The Leavenworth *Times*, where he was no doubt remembered, wrote, "he led a wild and reckless life, visiting gambling dens and raising disturbances wherever he went...his fate was well deserved." Those reporters weren't familiar with "Graham's Luck," but at least one writer for the Rocky Mountain News[118] interviewed Graham on his deathbed. Graham may have been "mortally wounded" but he was well enough to create a ridiculous story regarding the crime.

He claimed that, owing to some local election, he went out with Dyck on a drunken lark. He challenged Capt. Irwin in a macho way and when Irwin declined to come

---

[117] Dyck (or Dick in some reports) was former station keeper of the No. 1 stage station on the Atchison Topeka and Santa Fe Railroad.
[118] Reprinted in the Lawrence (KS) *Daily Journal*, Sept 18, 1873.

out of the ambulance, Graham and accomplice somehow managed to shoot three innocent people. Of course it was a coincidence that the transport was carrying a large sum of cash and was on a route former officer Graham was familiar with. In an insight into Graham's sociopathic way of manipulating people, he asked why on earth would he and one other person try to hold up twelve people? One could imagine feeling pity for a poor, dying man who took the labored breaths to ask a legitimate question.

However, two days after running Graham's deathbed interview, the Rocky Mountain *News* obtained some interesting info that pretty much sealed the case and made a mockery of Graham's excuse. The soldiers at the same camp Brooks was en route had been visited by the former Major, who ate, slept, and hung out with soldiers. A man from Fort Wallace's quartermaster office had been in Denver and probably talked about things he shouldn't have. According to this civilian, Graham knew that Brooks was on his way, so Graham and Dyck employed Graham's biggest talent and stole a few horses. They then rode to an area near a hill where they knew the pay ambulance would have to pass, and waited. The intent, according to this latest report, was to take the whole thing by surprise. Dyck managed to jump on the ambulance and put a pistol to the driver's head, but the driver kicked the mules into a gallop and Dyck fired his pistol, hitting the driver. Graham meanwhile aimed his shotgun at Irwin, hitting him in the back. They then tried to overtake the mules leading the ambulance and throw those animals into confusion. As Graham aimed his shotgun at the team, Wetmore drew his pistol and fired at Graham, who dropped like a sack of flour. If Wetmore, the only armed member, had not had that weapon the whole team may have been slaughtered, with Graham and Dyck committing cold-blooded murder for a total of $2000.

The feud with Irwin was also cleared up. Despite the fact that he was a disgraced former officer with no business on any Army post, Graham had tried to make himself at home at the post at River Bend. Capt. Irwin did not take kindly to a cashiered civilian, calling himself "Major" and helping himself to meals and a bed. He told the vagabond to stay away from the post, eventually running him off. Predictably, Graham threatened a nasty revenge.

As the story was picked up nationwide, local reporters discovered even more details on Graham's background. The Rocky Mountain *News* opined that Graham had been around Denver for at least a year, doing not much of anything besides hanging around in gambling dens. They did mention his cashiering but not any details, as the specifications of his court-martial were already being forgotten, or at least brushed aside. He was remembered by the Colorado *Daily Chieftain* as, among other things, "a genteel loafer and blackguard" and transgressor. Other journalists used such archaic terms for Graham as "footpad." Where was Graham planning to hide after the robbery? The crime wasn't terribly far from Kit Carson, could he have been planning to hide at Annie King's?

On the 17th an even more shocking bit of info came to light: Graham resorted to robbing a U.S. Paymaster *after* his plan to abscond with $800,000 from the U.S Mint failed. Not long before the paymaster incident, two treasury agents came into town escorting that amount, and Graham somehow learned that it was going to be stored in the mint in transit. He'd tried to get accomplices to help him steal it, but even the criminals he associated himself with were doubtful, especially since armed soldiers accompanied the agents.[119] Graham was now counting on a softer touch in the way of an unarmed pay coach.

After being shot Graham sent a wire to an "eclectic physician," Dr. S. W. Treat. Eclectic medicine was a form of treatment that relied on natural herbs for cures and pain management instead of bleeding, leeches, dangerous poisons, etc. Deputy U.S. Marshal Salisbury brought Graham back to Denver by train, along with three guards, two soldiers and one officer, all of the 6th Cavalry, who no doubt had dined with Graham the previous few months. Salisbury wanted to take the prisoner to the county jail but Graham's condition earned him a spot in a hospital. Noted Arapahoe County physician Dr. John Elsner examined Graham before giving a reporter permission to interview the patient.[120] The interview went as follows:

> --Reporter: "Major, I came for the express purposes of hearing whether you had any statement to make relative to that shooting affair."
>
> Graham: "I have not seen anything that has yet been published."
>
> Reporter: " Nothing so far has been published except the facts of the affair as they transpired."
>
> Graham: "Oh, it was all a drunken row, the effects of election day. Irwin had been on a spree for two weeks. I had been drinking with them and, on the day previous to the affair, a row had come up, in consequence of which they wanted me to fight Irwin at fifteen paces. I refused to do that."
>
> Reporter: "But what had that row to do with the paymaster and the attack on the wagon?"
>
> Graham: "Nothing whatever. I only wanted to call Irwin out of the wagon to fight me there and then. It is not likely that two men would attack twelve with the object of robbery."

At this point Graham grew too weak to continue, but before Dr. Elsner could leave, "no less than General G. W. Chamberlain walked in." This was George W. Chamberlain, former Attorney General of the Colorado Territory, removed from office in 1869 but still in Denver as a lawyer whose office was very close to Graham's room at a boarding house. Whether they knew each other or Chamberlain was a lawyer in search of headlines is unknown. Chamberlain would take the dying man's hand and tell him to sleep, and all would be fine, he was there for him.[121]

The *Tribune* noted that patients claimed Graham was walking around the hospital when his doctor was away. Dr. Elsner answered that this was impossible: Graham was mortally wounded. Marshal Salisbury stated that nevertheless, the patient was under constant watch by day and guard by night. He was said to be unable to eat and was not permitted visitors.

Other sources said that no guards were placed at Graham's room at the Arapahoe County Hospital because he had suffered a mortal gunshot. Nurses would report that for two weeks Graham seemed to linger on the edge of life and death and that

---

[119] Rocky Mountain *News*, September 11, 1873.
[120] The Jewish Museum of the American West reports that Elsner created first County Hospital in a small building at 9th and Mariposa Streets with 29 beds, the hospital being mattresses on boxes.
[121] Rocky Mountain *News*, Sept 14, 1873.

visitors were allowed. What was the truth? Were editors, eager to sell papers, cooking up a story of an invincible man? Locals were very worried that the desperado would escape, but were reassured that he was far too sick to simply get up and leave his bed.

Really? On Sept 24th, Graham's hospital bed was found empty. Another manhunt for Graham was underway. Reporters and citizens chastised the police for not keeping guard on a would-be murderer, as well as the dying man "probably being spirited away by men in a wagon while they (officials) were asleep."[122] The amazing story was picked up as far as New York where the *Gouverneur Times* reported that no guards were placed on him and he was allowed visitors. They also reported that half a dozen men had come in and helped him escape in a waiting carriage.[123] Clearly the claims that guards were lax and visitors allowed were true, as well as the story which appeared just once, that Graham was up and about behind his doctor's back. A Mr. Williams, who ran the hospital, claimed that no one but doctors were allowed into his room, yet the day after the escape the public learned that the previous Saturday a trunk was taken into Graham's room to give him a change of clothing, and returned to the house where he was a boarder three days later. That same night he escaped, apparently with the help of six other men and a female. Another patient claimed to have heard noises that night, and a different person said that six men carried Graham out. Dyck was reportedly seen back in Denver that Tuesday but vanished again, next turning up in Las Animas at the end of September, trying to get his horse reshod in only a few minutes. When told it was impossible Dyck told the blacksmith to "go to hell" and rode off. The 6th Cavalry, desperately trying to catch him, followed his trail but lost him.

Two days later H. C. Sherman, a Denver policeman, was patrolling Holladay Street[124] in the evening when he noticed an odd fellow ambling about in a hunched over manner. The man was tall, black, and wearing an old Army jacket meant for a private, and acted as if he were trying to avoid the newly installed gaslights. The strange fellow's hair stood out in a mess, and though thin and frail, his cheeks were plumped out. The officer walked ahead of the strange man to get a better look under a lamp and realized he might actually be white. Sherman stopped the character upon reaching I (18th) Street and asked the person his name. The answer given was Jim Brown. Jim said he lived near Holladay and I Streets, but pointed in the wrong direction.[125] Sherman steered the man into a nearby saloon, yanked off his wig and shirt, but still found dark skin. The hat on Jim's head, however, left a mark indicating the dark skin was mere makeup.

Then time stood still for but a second that could have made all the difference, as both men thought of reaching for Jim's pocket. Sherman reached into it first and found a revolver, along with a bottle of brandy. Once unarmed, the man said, "It is no use now. I'll tell you who I am. I am Graham." Graham then offered to bribe Sherman with $300 "within twenty minutes" in exchange for letting him go. Sherman replied that he was not the type of policeman to be bribed. Graham pleaded, saying he would not harm him, and offered that Sherman could simply tell his superiors that Graham had overpowered him and ran away. It did him no good for he was immediately on his way to jail.

---

[122] Chicago *Daily Tribune*, Oct 12, 1873
[123] October 15, 1873 edition.
[124] Now Market St.
[125] The Rocky Mountain *News* reported that Graham told Sherman he was on his way to 19th St. to get a change of clothes.

Sherman proudly paraded his capture along Larimer Street. Luckily for future historians, a writer was hanging around an area known as Feuerstein's Block when Sherman announced, "I've got him!" When the local asked who it was the officer shouted, "Graham!" The writer was confused, as the officer was not dragging Graham, but a lanky black man. The citizen approached the officer and his prize, noticing that, despite the masterful makeup (burnt cork) and sans his famous moustache, it was indeed Graham. Word spread in minutes on the street that the dying man/escapee was not only caught, but was here on the street, and a crowd gathered. The onlookers followed Sherman and Graham on the entire walk to the jail, and heard the incredible story firsthand as Sherman retold it.[126]

The wounded Graham would spend some time in the Arapahoe County Jail awaiting a trial. When asked by reporters how he managed to survive, "brandy" was his answer. Graham had accomplices in Denver who smuggled liquor to him before sneaking him out. Papers speculated that any others involved in the whole robbery/hospital escape story would be found but apparently never were. Naturally people asked how he escaped from the hospital, but Graham refused to name accomplices. He was defiant in stating that he escaped with no one's help. Whether it was loyalty or marketing himself as an amazing specimen of life is unknown. He did confess his plans though. After leaving his hospital bed he spent one day in town and a night in a barn, hoping to make his way to the depot in disguise, to take the Kansas Pacific Railroad out of town. How would he have quickly obtained $300 for that bribe? He was either lying or had accomplices after all. If it was his own money why did he not have it on him to help with his getaway? Or was he not even trying to get out of town? Considering his dishonesty there could have been another story. Newspapers were beginning to sense he was a liar and suspected that he may have had arranged for friends to wait for him with a wagon to leave town. He did make one last, pathetic statement from his new bed at the jailhouse: "I have no friends, and the public have condemned me without knowing the facts." This just continued Graham's act of being a victim of circumstance, except for the first time, the public wasn't buying it. He was having a hard time explaining the attempted robbery of an Army paymaster.

Staff noticed that Graham washed off the black disguise covering most of his body with no difficulty. The wound seemed to make little difference to his movements despite later comments that he would have a 4" scar on his back from it.

The superhuman that had cheated death and known for his escapes was housed in the first cell near the entrance in the jail, under guard it was assured. He was reported as saying next to nothing to other people and gave off an air of pity, his face seeming even more emaciated by the loss of his moustache.

The Rocky Mountain Detective Association, of which Sherman was a member, congratulated itself in the capture.

The consensus was that Graham had been part of a gang that may have been involved in a rash of burglaries the previous summer. One such robbery involved the country treasurer and his wife awaking to find their very bedroom had been robbed of jewelry and other items, including the man's keys to the safe in the city building. Upon discovering the missing keys officials rushed to the Hughes Block office where, sure

---

[126] Denver Daily *Times*, Sep 27, 1873.

enough, the safe had been opened and ransacked.[127] The thieves were, as far as I found, never caught. The keys were recovered where they had been thrown: a recently built German church.

Awaiting his fate, Graham saw the beginning of a newspaper war over him. Most papers reported the facts, along with describing Graham as slippery, criminal, desperate, and such. However the Denver *Mirror*, run by one Stanley G. Fowler, took a different view. Fowler, a native of Connecticut and Yale classmate of Senator Orville Piatt and known for his melodramatic writing style, blew into town earlier from Chicago. Fowler's *Mirror* became more obnoxious over the years regarding Graham, even taunting its perceived enemies into lawsuits. Fowler made no secret that he found Graham a sympathetic and misunderstood soul, taking him under his wing and giving readers a point of view they wouldn't see in those "other papers. One mention of Graham in his publication calls the thief "abused and vilified," arguing that his past glorious services should render any "misdeeds" paid in full. (Whether Fowler printed these articles because he truly fell for Graham's sociopathy, or was just giving a different view to sell his paper is unclear, but for Fowler to state that anything Graham did, including murder, should be overlooked because he had been a Civil War officer shows Fowler had a twisted point of view also).

Fowler conveniently ignored the fact that Graham was a disgraced hero, stripped and cashiered, labeled unfit for any office of public trust. He attacked any competing newspapers that were honest about Graham, even accusing those papers of wanting to try, hang and quarter this victim of circumstance. One can justify this by reckoning that Fowler was only hearing what Graham told him, and of course, Fowler wanted to sell papers by creating even more of a controversy regarding his new pet. But Fowler, commonly known as a great journalist, either did not dig up the truth on Graham or refused to do so. He wanted to dwell upon what this hero did before the cashiering, and not his recent crimes in Utah and Colorado. The slightest criticism of the *Mirror* incited Fowler. When the *Central Register* wrote, tongue-in-cheek, that they had committed a sin by speaking disrespectfully of Graham, Fowler asked for the "wounded, friendless and helpless victim to get a fair show," and since Graham was charged with only three of seven charges, this was proof that he was not a robber or highwayman.

On Oct 12, 1873, the *Mirror* ran its own interview with Graham. This reporter, possibly Fowler himself, would not subject the prisoner to questions that would tire and weaken him. This was a longer interview, showing how Graham felt much better when given the right questions, or rather when he smelled a prospective sympathizer with media connections. Graham was becoming what we would now call a media whore, using the press to his advantage, manipulating the one editor and ally who sold papers by printing a different version of the story and forming a symbiotic relationship. Indeed, on the 14th, the Daily Colorado *Chieftain* strongly hinted that Graham was paying Fowler off.

The *Mirror* pointed out that Graham, once captured, took his punishment meekly "like a struck calf." Remember that, when he was caught, Graham attempted to draw his gun on Sherman, and only walked off like a baby animal when that gun was pointed at him. Fowler labeled Graham an underdog who was being torn apart by large bulldogs (rival newspapers). In this interview the jail itself is painted as Dante's Hell, one step above a medieval torture chamber. The only thing missing from Fowler's description is a

---

[127] Denver Daily Times. Jul 10, 1873.

sweaty man forging implements over a fire. Major Graham then made his appearance, eager to shake hands in that gentlemanly way, apologizing as he went to sit but stopped to adjust his clothing in a show of discomfort. Fowler always referred to the accused and later convicted as Major Graham, sans quotation marks, and from the feel of it all one can imagine Fowler practically genuflecting in his presence. Fowler's description alternates between gushing and tear-jerking: slender but strong hands, large gray eyes, his thin face not showing any of the brutality he must be tolerating in that hell-hole with a quiet and dignified manner. Even his lips are described and the whole face of Graham, who looked the interviewer in the eye as he spoke, could not possibly be that of a "ruffian." He would no doubt look death straight in the face as well, and is definitely a well-bred gentleman, not even uttering a curse word. Let's recall Harriet's letter, desperate for info on her boy, whom she admitted was always in trouble.

The writer then tells us in his mawkish way that our highly dignified prisoner complained of his wound, suffers shortness of breath and weakness, despite the fact that policemen noticed that he had no difficulty whatsoever washing off his disguise and changing. Fowler claimed that the man was far too sick to be held in this dungeon, ignoring the fact that Graham, in worse shape, escaped from a low security hospital bed. Another headshaking statement informs *Mirror* readers that Graham has always limited himself, acquaintance wise, to real gentlemen, scions of society, and would never, ever brag on himself. Was Fowler living in the same city where Graham had been making a reputation as a pest? Regarding his modesty, Fowler noted, he only speaks of war heroics when pressed. This is where any modern reader must suspend belief. The former officer who swaggered about New Bern as "The Hero of the War" was actually a bastion of modesty? Astonishingly, Graham complained that he only escaped from the hospital as part of a plot by other newspapers to malign him to the public and he didn't want horrible stories to get back to his "poor mother." Recall that Harriet had so rarely heard from her son that she had been forced to ask for help in finding him.

Graham told the interviewer that he though could hunt Indians and command a cavalry troop, he was simply not accustomed to such treatment from the press. This was believable as Graham had been a media delight for years and now he had to face the truth in print instead of seeing his exploits hailed as bravery. He was of course making claims that the press was meaner to him than any enemy ever was. He was also behind bars, not in a field at sunset contemplating which town he would pillage that night.

The *Mirror* then claimed to beg Graham for a packet of papers, the famous scrapbook with recommendations, but surely no court-martial records. Graham made a show of false modesty but of course he was "persuaded" to present it. Why he had it in jail, or for that matter how the reporter even knew of its existence is odd. What the scrapbook did not show, Graham gladly filled in the blanks. He lied through his teeth when he told the reporter that he had been a private who worked his way up to a lieutenant colonel. The actual commission of December 1861 to 2nd Lt. was enclosed but no one questioned the absence of documents of Graham as a private. Then he claimed to have risked his life to save Gen. Wessels, but pretended to be too shy to recount heroics but made damned sure the reporter knew about them. For a modest man who hated publicity, his collection containing those old glowing newspaper clippings stayed with him no matter where he fled. More documents were brought out by the humble prisoner, with the *Mirror* to boasting that they contained signatures by the likes of President Grant. Of course the President would have signed promotions of any officer, but this was all made to sound like

Grant singled out Graham. Recommendations for a brevet lieutenant colonel were mentioned, but not enclosed were the refusals.

(Later, when he went to prison, he stated that his place of birth was North Carolina. Graham must have been sticking to his lie that he was from the south but went north at the outbreak of war. The lies had caught up. In his scrapbook were enlistment papers showing Crown Point as residence, but also recommendations from A.K. Long listing Graham as a good southern boy. The scoundrel had told so many lies that he had to combine them. Fowler never mentioned these contradictions in his newspaper).

On Oct 18 Graham pled not guilty to the third, sixth and seven counts.[128] It was a busy day for pleas, but Graham must have been the star of the Indictment Parade, outshining the likes of a Mr. Suitterlin for example, arraigned that day for misusing the post office in a phony lottery scam. Did Suitterlin and others awaiting arraignment look up and down at the main subject of the local papers? In those papers, Graham was made out to be the anti-Christ.

But was he actually JUST a pest and not much else?

Court transcripts turned up in the Denver Archives are interesting, to say the least. The actual testimony is written in old Pitman legalese shorthand and cannot be read until someone is found who can transcribe them.

However, another stack of papers IS in regular writing. Bad, but readable.

The trial dates had to be postponed, over someone's illness, getting a witness here and there, etc. Graham's attorneys were trying to get a mistrial declared once it did begin. Salisbury was allowed to pick the jury! Those jurors came from areas that the crime did not occur in, and some didn't even live in Denver. The DA told the jury not to take anything Graham said into consideration. Add to this the odd case itself, the US vs G. W. Graham and John Dick, et al. George and his alleged accomplice were tried at the same time, same case, and what was "et al" about? That referred to any person or persons unknown who helped Graham escape from the hospital. Trying an unknown number of unknown people in absentia…amazing.

H. C. Alleman, for the Territorial Government of Colorado, wrote out directions to the case, including such official directions that "it is not necessary to prove an actual conspiracy, but it may be inferred." One of the charges was conspiracy, but they did not have to prove it. Another along the same lines, when charging Graham with conspiracy with John Dick, it was "not necessary to prove any direct connect, or even any meeting, of the conspirators."

It was as if Denver was going to make a point of Graham no matter what. Need more proof? Rule 10 in the DA's instructions to the jury was "Circumstantial evidence is equally as strong as direct evidence…"

The court held itself untouchable regarding the absence of Dick, and said it is no way a negative reflection of the court that he was being tried in absentia. Graham was to

---

[128] The counts and all details are unknown. I've searched with the help of the folks at the Denver Archives but nothing has been unearthed.

testify dead last, and there was no rebuttal permitted. He asked for twenty instructions through his attorney. Every single one was refused. One, for example, was that if they jury did find a conspiracy, they should have to state what that conspiracy was and that it match the charges. Makes sense, but it was refused. Graham also asked that it be proved beyond a reasonable doubt. Refused. Considering that Dick was never captured, any shooting cannot be proved to have been from his gun. Refused. When proving that the motive that night was robbery, the jury should take into consideration the number of people in the ambulance and the unlikeliness of two men to take on that many officers. Refused. Apparently the government brought the Fourteenth Amendment into the case. It almost sounds like what we call today a "hate crime" in that, because the ambulance carried a U.S. paymaster, the severity of the count of conspiracy to rob the government was that much worse. Part of the Fourteenth Amendment referred to was that any government employees or officials were in danger of their lives because of "unfriendly attitude" by the "people of the Southern States." Graham argued that nothing in the Fourteenth Amendment, or anything concerning the South or Reconstruction had anything to do with this case. Refused.

George maintained that he was drunk that evening after the affair at Camp River Bend (probably like everyone else) and was angry at being thrown out of camp by Irwin. It does ring true; he had a very short temper. So, he argued, he had heard that Irwin was out near the Hugo train station and would be back by daybreak. Somewhere he ran into this John Dick fellow, who lived nearby, and who was also mad as hell that people were stealing his buffalo hides as they hung out to dry. This was going on systematically, and despite Dick's absence, Graham told Dick's side of the story. Dick had been drinking himself, and waiting in the area for thieves to show up, telling Graham he was going to "ku klux" them. This old term meant several things, but in this context Dick was probably planning to beat them up and/or disarm them. It is notable that not one witness from Dick's area near Hugo was brought in to testify about gangs stealing property at night.

On the day of sentencing the courtroom was packed. People wanted to see the man who cheated death.

The U.S. District Attorney for Colorado, Hiram C. Alleman[129], made closing arguments that Saturday morning before Judge Ebenezer Wells[130] spoke to the jury.

They were out longer than anyone anticipated and must have given Graham the feeling that he was to be freed, especially since the unpretentious defendant produced during the trial his scrapbook. Former Attorney General Chamberlain may have sat at his side, for Graham's attorneys are lost to history.

As the verdicts of guilty on the charge of conspiracy and two others were read aloud reporters noted that Graham went "deathly pale," momentarily losing his composure but quickly changing back to the smooth persona he'd adopted. His attorneys motioned for a new trial, but Graham was on his way to the new Colorado Territorial Prison with a sentence of two years and a $1000 fine.[131] The Denver *Daily Times* was as much

---

[129] Alleman was a Civil War colonel and had been in charge of Gettysburg Battlefield right after the bloodshed.
[130] Coincidentally, Wells had been appointed in 1872 by Pres. Grant, the same man who endorsed Graham into the regular army, and signed his court-martial papers.
[131] Daily State *Journal*, Alexandria VA. Nov 26, 1873

concerned with a female reporter's summation of how well dressed the jury was, indeed it wasn't just any reporter; it was Sara Jane Clark, aka Grace Greenwood, the first female reporter for the New York *Times*, known for her travel pieces from the American West, as well as Europe. Clark had traveled to Colorado for the trial. The motion was denied a week later and newspaper banter continued. The Rocky Mountain *News* sent a semi-transparent message to the *Mirror* by way of a Graham update, ending it, "Finally, we remark that the attempt to manufacture sympathy for him by publishing one side of his army record, would fall that were both sides told at the same time."

John Suitterlin, arraigned the same day as Graham, was also found guilty and was convicted and sentenced to the same lockup. Both men had time to play catch up as they were transported together to Pueblo, then taken to Canon City on Dec 3. It was not their plan...found in their shared cell after they were taken to Cañon City was a fresh hole in the floor, large but covered. In it was a small knife, serrated like a saw. One or both men had been planning an escape! The two jailbirds had one hell of a sense of humor about the whole thing. Suitterlin had wallpapered their cell with newspaper ads of his mail order scam, and over the door of the cell the men posted a sign reading "For Sale or to Rent." There's an item your author would love to have in her collection.

The Colorado Territorial Prison was new and somewhat isolated. Major Graham was now just known as prisoner number 75.

Pacing the room constantly, his restless nature could not bear a lock up. Like a caged panther he obsessed on a way out. The panther quickly made a few friends, one being his companion on the trip from Denver, John Suitterlin, but the other was not a white-collar man convicted of misusing the postal system, but the convicted axe murderer George Witherell. By 1874 one of Graham's Gang admitted they were waiting for warm weather to make their break. Graham, a perpetual illness faker, would be the "diversion."

The warden was already on alert. He sensed a break was imminent and ordered cells to be searched. In both Witherell's and Graham's cells, rags containing matches sewn in were discovered. A brick in Graham's cell sat at an odd angle, and was found to be removable and was obviously a cache for something now missing. Graham had been questioned about it and calmly showed the questioners a file. Mr. Hines, a former prison guard, according to Graham, had given the file to him. The papers stated that Hines, for $400, would enable Graham to escape. Graham obtained the money from home in North Carolina but Hines then asked for another couple hundred. Graham showed the interrogator a letter from his sister corroborating his asking for $400 but needing no more as the chance to buy his way out had passed. The investigator should have done a more thorough examination of his cell. Graham apparently had one sister in North Carolina.

A few days later the warden was making plans to release a prisoner identified as Ryan. Ryan warned the warden that the night guard should be on extra watch.

Just after midnight on May 26th Graham made a show of doubling over, groaning and writhing from abdominal pains. The guard on their floor quickly went to upstairs to obtain some laudanum, a tincture of opium. Ryan and Witherell let themselves out of their cells with a homemade key. They then threw a blanket over the guard, who managed to shove one prisoner away. Witherell struck the guard with such force it knocked him out cold, enabling the prisoners to tie and gag him. They then took his keys and helped themselves to food, blankets, guns and ammunition, and changed into civilian clothes from the premises. Before leaving they tried to free more prisoners, who refused to escape. They fled into the darkness of a tranquil Colorado night, perhaps helped by an almost full moon.

Locals would begin their day by hearing of the escape, and so many conflicting reports were spread by word of mouth that it was hard to get the facts. A description of the criminals from prison records was posted in newspapers[132], noting that Graham was 6'1", weighed about 165 pounds, and had scars from gunshots on a finger of his left hand and his right side. No mention was made of the large scar on his back from the paymaster robbery attempt. A few of his partners had shot wounds as well: Graham may have put on airs as a charmer but sought out the lowlifes in his travels. Two days later a letter from Warden Rudd to the governor was discovered in which Rudd tells Acting Governor Jenkins that the convicts escaped with plenty of Spencer carbines, and did indeed possess a homemade key. (Witherell had demonstrated a talent for this upon his last arrest). Rudd, while warning that the convicts were well armed, opines that the gang was most likely headed for Texas, if not across the border entirely. On the first day of June the *Mirror* ran actual letters from Graham and Suitterlin explaining their escape, excusing it because of cruel torture at the Colorado Territorial Prison on the part of former management but praising the current one. It is remarkable that they broke out under an administration they complimented. Graham also made another claim: someone working in the prison had robbed him of money. Three days later the follow-ups noted not this particular item, but that Graham's allegations should be looked into and anyone disagreeing with the investigation must be guilty.[133] Besides Witherell and Suitterlin, the escape party consisted of George Millsap and Fred Downing: robbers, Thomas Mason: swindler, Charles Yetter and John Ryan: grand larceny. Newspapers such as the *Daily Chieftain* stressed that they blamed no one in particular but could not overlook past claims of mismanagement that should be investigated.

Warden Rudd sent off a dispatch to Jenkins asking if he could offer a reward to which Jenkins replied that $500 was accepted.

Graham's cell was inspected once again, this time a chisel and saw were found and niches had been drilled between bricks to hide other tools, tools that were gone, with the holes covered and whitewashed. In dramatic flair Graham left a note for the warden, who stated that he felt Graham and Witherell were probably attempting to make it to Mexico or at least Texas but would not be taken alive.

Rosita, forty miles south of Canon City, was a mining town in the Wet Mountain Valley. In 1863 gold and silver were found in the area, and by 1872 the Hardscrabble Mining District was established. The town began to boom. The same year of the escape, the Pocahontas and Humboldt mines were sending ore out by carloads. James Pringle from Scotland was a pioneer of Rosita and an example of the mixture of American and foreign blood in the non-silver veins of the town. It was a friendly, hard working area with beautiful views, but also a town containing the expected seeds of trouble regarding boundaries and claims.

---

[132] Canon City *Times*, May 28, 1874.
[133] Canon City *Times*, June 4, 1874.

On a Monday morning in June, four prospectors from San Juan stopped over to buy food before going to the Sangre de Christo Pass. A miners' meeting was held that night, nothing odd about that, and had been earlier advertised. What would be notable about that meeting was the discovery the following morning. One by one residents noticed that, while they were gathered at the meeting the night before, their homes had been looted. It didn't take a genius to figure out who the prospectors really were, especially when the stolen items were things like arms, clothes and cooking pans. Resident John Johnson even had his suit stolen and neighbor Mr. Bradbury had some expensive boots taken. They also broke into the home of pioneer James Pringle and stole the popular man's revolver.

Locals feared for themselves as the well-known and wicked Graham, along with seven other criminals was somewhere in the area. Search parties went out, no doubt armed to the teeth. On June 8 word was out that the escapees were spotted in Rosita posing as miners. That night, it would be discovered, the gangsters all went to cabins in the mountains west of town. Twelve men, including guards Paul Ross and Elroy Packard, and citizens James Pringle and another named Thornton, set out to find the escapees. All was quiet until some young boys from Rosita, out with the guards, heard rumblings of men at an empty cabin a few miles away. A postal carrier also learned from someone that four strangers now inhabited the old Jones cabin, south of Rosita.

Overnight the guards and the others found the cabin near a tributary of Antelope Creek. Situating themselves among large rocks, they waited silently in the dark with weapons ready. An occasional flicker of the fireplace indoors could be seen and the escapees switched watch every couple of hours. The sun had just come up facing the mountains when it happened. It was Graham's turn at watch. He appeared outside the cabin door, stretching and carrying a carbine. A witness who went by "MDC" reported that Graham looked fearless and "proud as an uncaged lion." His demeanor changed, as he seemed to have sensed the clicks from the hidden gunmen because he tried to draw, but it was too late. After the shooting stopped Graham was down, mortally wounded with bullets in his spine and neck, only uttering a few words, telling "his men" not to come out. Thomas Mason approached the door next and was shot in the stomach. Only two more of the gang had been holed up in the cabin, Witherell and Milsap, who both surrendered. The limp bodies of Graham and Mason were hauled off to Rosita, tended to by a doctor, and returned to the prison. Witherell and Milsap were quickly taken to the penitentiary. The remaining four convicts were still loose, with Packard now going after them with a party from Rosita. One of the four captured men still had the key used to make their escape. Warden Rudd proudly took the key, noting it was roughly made but did the job. Rosita awoke to the good news and the townspeople (with a few exception) were said to have been "rejoicing."[134] The reports made a story once again of Graham's fall from grace and everything leading up to this final ending. Much was made of his being the only man to escape after an assault on a Mormon girl in Salt Lake City and his escape from an angered father's gun. The same article[135] writes that George Witherell, "if possible, was a far worse man even than Graham, a true cold-blooded killer." Whereas Graham the charmer-criminal had friends, Witherell was truly without anyone to vouch for him.[136]

---

[134] *Inter-Ocean* (Chicago), June 17, 1874.
[135] Ibid
[136] Witherell would eventually meet a grisly death. The details are at the end of this book.

There was no opinion from Fowler's *Mirror* regarding the Mormon incident, but Fowler had a point when he wrote of his outrage at Graham being shot full of holes by a sneak ambush at the cabin, after all, pointed out Fowler, Graham had not been sentenced to death and the men who waited all night for him to emerge had no business playing judge and executioner.

Who were the exceptions not celebrating his shooting and recapture? The Daily Rocky Mountain *News* told its readers on June 17th that "two or three young women, worshippers of the blood and thunder heroes of ten cent novels, have carried bouquets to him every day." The young women bringing flowers to Graham on his presumed deathbed in Rosita have never been identified.

A few details emerged from Rosita on the arrival of Graham and his "miners" in that town. Graham had visited a Mr. Leary, and it appeared Graham claimed to lay out a stage route from Canon City. It was Leary who mentioned to Graham that a meeting would be held that night in the town hall, so Graham's gang walked into unlocked cabins and helped themselves to food, weapons, clothing and anything else they wanted.[137]

Newspapers began running the second of Graham's obituaries. Just like the year before, he was on his deathbed but quite capable of giving another newspaper interview. He did not talk very much, this time in considerable pain, but acknowledged that he had sent two letters to the *Mirror* regarding his torture.[138] He also admitted that he gave Rice $50 to pay a debt and another $150 to pay off a Washington lawyer who was trying to secure a pardon. Frequent sick leave for personal use in his Civil War days must have given him the confidence to play the sympathy card after his cashiering. He gave that first ridiculous interview to the *Mirror* after being shot near River Bend, faked illness in prison so well that a guard left his post to get medicine thus enabling an escape, and now the dying victim once again gave a pitiful, self-serving spiel to the public via his willing mouthpiece: the *Mirror*. Incredibly, he also claimed that they did not technically do anything wrong by looting homes in Rosita. Graham said that the citizens would have given them what they wanted had they simply asked. No one dared put it to Graham that if that were true, they would not have waited until the homes were unoccupied.

What were these letters that had the public so fascinated? Both were written on June 15, 1874 from Canon City. One, written by Suitterlin and endorsed by Witherell was a statement. Suitterlin claimed that around the New Year, prison employee Mr. James Hines took Graham from his cell and said that for $400 he would supply him with the tools to escape. For $500 Hines would enable Suitterlin to escape as well. Hines allegedly told Suitterlin that he would give a false personal description and send any officials in the opposite direction when hunting down the men. Suitterlin goes on to say that he was expecting a pardon and would not go along with the plot. (He did otherwise). Time passed and Warden Rudd was now in charge, and though the prisoners claimed to have no ill will towards Rudd, they awaited warm weather to make their break, with tools and keys that Suitterlin claimed Hines had reneged on giving the men. The totally trustworthy George

---

[137] Colorado *Daily Chieftain*, June 14, 1874.
[138] Former Superintendent C S Reed asked to see these letters, claiming they were forged by Rudd to make him look bad.

Witherell signed a handwritten certificate stating he was with Graham when the latter mailed two letters to Fowler at the *Mirror* address.

Also in June Fowler began referring to former superintendent Reed as "the old devil" and claims that Reed and his former administration were the real criminals, and bemoaned the "betrayal" of Graham and his gang, supposedly for not helping in their escape. Yet on June 28, Fowler's paper ran another deathbed interview in which Graham states that he paid Hines $400 for his escape. Graham also stated that the bump on the guard's head put there by Witherell was from the "timid man falling over a chair." According to the dying prisoner, they had spent eight days on the other side of the hill from the Territorial Prison before making their way south to Rosita by way of the mountains west of the bridge (possibly River Gorge). In this latest obituary, The *Mirror* wrote that should Graham survive, he should wait out his term, shun liquor, and live a good life.

The poor fellow even had another letter from sister Mattie, this one mailed to Fowler himself. Being the total journalist Fowler obviously was, he would only write bits of the letter, a letter proving what a misunderstood man Graham was. The following is verbatim.

> -- He is dearer to me now in his humiliation and trouble than ever before. Poor fellow, he has been more sinned against than sinning. If you will do what you can (without injury to yourself), to secure from him some memento, if it comes in the worst, believe me I shall be deeply grateful…I would start to-night to go to him, but have not the means. I do not wish you to think that I ever believed Graham guilty of the crime they charge him with. No indeed, there's nothing on earth would make me believe it but his own assertion. May God reward you for your prompt attention to my letter, and the kind feeling you have manifested toward him. May you never have as heavy a heart as I have to-night. I see him ever before my eyes - shot down like a dog – wounded, bleeding, dying, and – I – am – here. --

Was this letter really from Mattie? Or was it actually from Josephine back in North Carolina?

Warden Reed earlier had quoted the *Mirror* as being a "pimp" for criminals. The *Mirror* never hesitated to paint Graham as an innocent, harmless gentleman and Graham honed in on its gullibility with his built-in radar. One *Mirror* column brags of Graham as a lover of women, and not in the sense that he had abandoned one wife and two children.

Regarding "Utah Nellie," Graham was asked about her, but he calmly replied in his manner that he would not mention her name, saying it would be a rude thing to do to a female. Remarks like that were enough to mesmerize Fowler into thinking that Graham was a true gentleman. A man with all the qualities to win over the country if he would only have one chance to prove himself: bravery, gentility, intelligence, breeding, daring, altruism, chivalrous to the ladies, and so on. One would like to ask Fowler if Graham hadn't had plenty of chances.

The *Rocky Mountain News*, never buying into Graham's victim-of-circumstance routine, ran a brief bio of Graham, almost referring to him as if he had died already. Indeed it looked as if he would not recover from these wounds.

A few years had passed since the Utah arrest so the *Rocky Mountain News* saw fit to inform the people of about Nellie Adams's rape charge and how much of it was dropped due to "contradictions." One item reported was that Graham had not just claimed to be a Southerner but that he had served on both sides in the Civil War. The paper reported his "natural gravitation" to lawlessness, and his narrow miss from a Mormon man's bullets gave him a new nickname: football of fortune, meaning someone whose personal fortunes inflate and deflate.

His second obituary ran in many newspapers but with more gossipy bits. Under the care of Dr. J. M. Bradbury (who'd who had his house robbed by Graham and gang in Rosita) and his own luck, Graham lived to tell the tale. These latest obits were the only mentions of the "certain drugs of a suspicious nature" purchased by Nellie. It had been three years past and no one cared to protect her anymore. But she and Graham's daughter were still in Salt Lake City, living with her mother and stepfather.

On June 18, 1874, the Denver *Mirror* ran one of the most preposterous columns yet on Graham. It states that military titles were passed out so often they were rendered cheap, and egomaniacs carrying those titles insisted on using them forever despite any evidence that they did not deserve them. Fowler was not talking about his pet though.

Fowler was actually picking a nasty fight with Maj. William W. Lander who was Denver Postmaster. Lander, a civilian from Massachusetts during the Civil War, was made a captain and brevet major by Gen. Benjamin Butler in the Commissary Subsistence Department of the Army. Lander also spent part of the war in North Carolina, possibly in a Colored Troops regiment. Fowler compared Lander to Graham, "a real Major who enlisted as a private and without friends or influence rose step by step to the rank of brevet major in the regular army." It goes on to describe Graham in the most dramatic and romantic way. The head of a band of cavalry "swooping down towards blood-thirsty savages," "always among the smoke of battle," and who was always in the heaviest of battles against Confederates, and was brave enough to drop the sword and gun and just beat them off, one by one, with his bare hands.

This article describing the difference between real and fake Majors (assuming he meant military versus civilian rank) ended with Fowler ripping into Butler for "giving clemency" to Lander.[139] As for Graham being "Hero of the Civil War" Fowler had no way of knowing that the few larger battles Graham was involved in were not by his choice, and that he was most known as a leader of looters and thieves, a hero of skirmishes usually ending with Graham being unable to resist burning any nearby church or house, self-serving by his frequent sick calls for personal business, and a his nighttime hobby of storming into homes while the men were away and robbing women and children.

It is impossible to know whether Fowler was taken in by Graham's personality or had some other mindset.

---

[139] In 1870 Lander was accused of misappropriating $6000 from his appointment as Postmaster of Salem, MA and then given the Denver assignment allegedly through friends in high places. The story of Fowler and Lander is deep, digging into President Grant's replacing of Colorado government figures with newbies, with Fowler going after those he considered part of a conspiracy to grab land and positions. Fowler had no ill will toward Grant over the latter's favoritism to Graham however.

Fowler's *Mirror* ran Graham's only known quotes about Nellie. When the *Rocky Mountain News* ran a Graham obit with part of the story of his trouble in Salt Lake City, Fowler wasn't happy, either because he missed the story, or because he did not want it known, yet a competitor got hold of it. Most papers were trying (with much success) to get at the truth of the notorious Graham, yet Fowler, granted total access to Graham, printed countless lies and myths about him. The Utah incident was, to quote Graham completely: "I do not feel at liberty to disclose her name. She is a lady of position. I never strove to conciliate her regard, but rather avoided her, for her husband was a kindhearted fellow and a good friend of mine."

Fowler took this as proof of Graham's chivalry without checking on the lady of position. He would have found that Nellie was never married, Graham had no real friends in Utah except lowlifes, and thus he probably claimed she had status to push his image that he only associated with the crème of society. The fact that she bore a child nine months after they admitted living together makes that short quote a set of four lies, as the man of honor was denying his own baby and claiming he spurned Nellie's attention. Only under months of aggressive research, a few lucky breaks, and the help of an archivist who went above and beyond, did I find the truth about Nellie and Graham's daughter, covered up and forgotten until 2015. Fowler could have found this in the 1870s but actively chose not to dig into Graham's past like any other journalist would, or maybe he did and found the truth was very different than what he had been printing. Fowler looked like a fool to some in Denver who did know part of the truth.

The *Mirror* was not finished knocking down anyone even slightly seen as some enemy to Graham. In Fowler's pretzel logic, the escape was Warden Reed's fault though Reed was gone by then, and that Rudd, the warden during the escape, could not be responsible because the keys used were made by someone else.

On that same day, June 18, the Canon City *Times* published something else that Fowler's pen never addressed: a long oath to a criminal gang found in Graham's clothing when recaptured. Here it is in its entirety:

>*--Rules and Regulations for the Government of the Liberty Band, and Iron Clad Boys.*

1st – *Courtesy and common civility shall guide us in our intercourse between another.*

2nd- *All disputes arising from any cause shall be settled by the Captain; or if he cannot settle them, by the whole band; Majority ruling. The course, distance and campground by the same.*

3rd- *All plunder or spoils shall be considered as company property, and disposed of as the Majority directs.*

4th- *Any member disobeying any of the above rules, or breaks the following oath, can be expelled by the Majority, and he shall forfeit all claim for protection or*

> *property in or from the band. All new rules or amendments can be added by a Majority vote of the whole band.*

> ### OATH
>
> *We, the undersigned, members of _____ band, do solemnly swear before Almighty God that we will abide by the rules, by-laws and regulations, and observe them in every instance, to the best of my knowledge and ability: That in cases where any of the members should by unforeseen circumstances get into trouble of any kind whatsoever, the remaining members shall do everything to free such member or members from such trouble. Every member shall be true to the others in all cases, and shall not betray any member or members under any circumstances, as he hopes for salvation or mercy in the other world. May our tongues cleave to the roof of our mouths should we in any manner betray any of the secrets of this organization. May God, who is all powerful, strike us dead the moment we go beyond the bounds of these sentiments. May the Devil and his imps take us the moment we I any way break these resolutions. Every man signing this paper does so knowing that the living God, who is the most powerful of all beings, is our witness and executor. We call upon the Almighty God to bear witness to every signature hereto affixed, knowing as he does that every member does so willingly and cheerfully, being aware of the punishment inflicted by the avenging hand should any member not observe this oath. May the yawning pit of Hell swallow us in her fiery furnace should we be willingly and knowingly break this oath, so help me God. Signed. Geo Wallace, Mike Connors, Chas Munglow, Wm St John, Scott Nelson, Frank Carr, Charles Henry, George Riley. –*

This is interesting on several levels. One, we have proof in his own hand that Graham was a gang leader and "sharing the spoils" obviously refers to anything stolen by the gang. The name of the gang was the Liberty Band and/or Iron Clad Boys. Was this an inside joke by leader Graham, referring to both the idea of prisoners being clad in irons and the ironclads he must have seen in North Carolina?

Who were these other men who signed the oath? A little investigation and some guesswork indicate that they were the same men Graham escaped with. "George Wallace" was simply Graham minus his surname and "Mike Connors" was probably John Ryan, as Ryan had boarded in Denver with a man named Mike O'Connell. William St. John? Likely John William Suitterlin who simply reworked his own name.

Found in his cell after the escape was a letter claimed to have been from Graham's sister, postmarked New Bern. A newspaper article from that city mentioned that he was from a "prominent local family" who was ashamed of him.[140] This letter mentioning a prominent family threw my research off until Graham's marriage was discovered. The family wasn't Graham's, but rather the John Fisher Jones family of Craven County, NC. Still, it does read like a blood relative. It is possible that Josephine went back to New Bern after Graham took off for the Territories. He must have been in contact with someone in

---

[140] *Daily Newbernian*, June 16, 1874. This family has not been identified and the story behind the mention is a mystery.

New Bern, as "Mattie" mentions here an offer to set up a business in New Bern. The Joneses were merchants, so it is not out of the question that an estranged wife or naïve sister may have written it.

Here is the unedited letter in its entirety.

--- Home, December 27, 1873

My dear, dear Brother: Your letter of the 8th instant came duly to hand, and oh, brother, why did you not write to us before? You gave me to understand all the time your case not a serious one and we are now by the papers (the Denver Mirror) that you were without friends and without money. This affair has almost killed mother, and makes her look ten years older. And oh, brother, I cannot realize the situation you are placed in. *We do not realize for one moment you are guilty of any crime that could place you where you are.* Command and instruct us what to do, and it shall be done. You say you will be released soon, but will not be able to come home at once. We will assist you with means to start into some business and you have friends here. You tell us in your letter not to write to you again while you are in that place. How is that? We don't understand you. It cannot be possible, dear brother, you do not wish to hear from us, for, brother, you have always been affectionate and good. You should certainly write to mother, for your letters would cheer her up much. We send this with a draft on New York city for four hundred ($400) to Mr. Hines, per instructions. If you want more you shall have it. Anything to release you from that dreadful place. Answer this, and tell me all about yourself. Our prayers ascend to Him daily that he, with his mercy, will restore you again to health and liberty. With mother's and my own love, I am ever your affectionate sister Mattie. ---

The letter was published in the Denver *Mirror* on May 27, 1874. The addition of the Denver *Mirror* in parentheses was obviously added by the editor, as well as the italics regarding his sister's belief in his innocence.[141] Graham may have wanted to keep only one trusted connection to his family, to have mail shipped to him via someone in New Bern, to get money if needed, or any other reason only known to him. In his prison records his mother is listed as Harriet Graham, living in New Bern, but unless Harriet visited a relative in New Bern it's another Graham invention. Harriet was a NY resident on the 1870 and 1875 New York censuses. Is it even possible that Fowler invented the letter?

Mystery Mattie's letter wasn't the only thing in the *Mirror* on that day regarding Graham, but it conveniently fit with Fowler's persistence that Graham was innocent of anything he had been caught red-handed doing. It had been argued by Fowler that Graham was not guilty of anything since he only *attempted* to rob a U.S Paymaster; he did not succeed. No sympathy was given in kind to Major Brooks, who suffered from a gunshot wound, or the other innocents who also sustained injuries.

The same day as Fowler ran Mattie's letter as pro-Graham propaganda, a few other lengthy items were printed. (One will never know if the public agreed or thought the

---

[141] Census records showing a Martha H Graham married a William K Johnson, Essex County, NY but there is no indication they ever resided in North Carolina.

Mirror was indeed a pimp. Fowler was enjoying a decent circulation probably because of human nature. People like to see competing media outlets fighting, and even if the average reader knew Graham was a scoundrel they were getting interviews not in other papers).

What of the letter to the warden Graham left on the night of his escape? The Mirror gleefully ran it on the same day as Mattie's letter. Here it is, also in its entirety, the blanks being illegible areas.

---Mr. Rudd

Sir: The only regret I have in leaving this place is the way I am about to, is, that it may make you and some of your officers trouble. One month ago I had no idea I would do this. The die is cast and I will go with the tide. The remaining tolls that Hines gave me I leave here in my cell; also, the letter from my sister, to show how I have been wronged. I will not assert that I will not be retaken, for all things are possible; but if I have a chance, I will give up my life first. I may regret this step all my life. I am not the ___ of this, neither ___. There are men in Colorado who have been active in placing me here, whom I never as long as I live will forgive. Your treatment of the prisoners here will have a tendency to keep more than locks and chains will. When I found out, a few days ago, that some of the convicts were determined to make a break, I advised as best I could not to use violence or hurt anyone and I hope now they will not. If they ___ as they promised, they would after they secure the night watchman, I shall try and not have them take as many with them as they now intend to. I shall not go with a crowd. Reed and his officers are responsible for the whole of this – the dogs. Respectfully G. W. Graham ---

Recall Graham's claim that he had barely a dollar to his name. According to the Honorable John B. Rice of the Prison Board, Graham enlisted Rice to use a draft to remove $200 from a business firm in New York and send $50 of it to Graham's wife in New Jersey, and bring him the balance. Rice took the draft to the First National Bank in Pueblo to await its clearing, after which he sent the money to New Jersey and left the balance in the bank. He was busy and could not get to Pueblo to collect the $150 to deliver to Graham, who carried on about it to Mr. Rudd. Rice finally just withdrew it and mailed it to Graham in care of the Canon City Penitentiary. Graham claimed he never received it. The Mirror attacked Rice, basically calling the noted man a liar, or perhaps simply an idiot for mailing cash. Rice shot back at the Mirror, stating that he did as he was asked and once it was in the mail it was not his problem. If Fowler questioned Graham about a wife, the conversation is lost, as the Mirror always maintained that Graham had never been married. Instead of looking at Graham's past, Fowler campaigned against Rice!

Fowler would never realize how striking that mention of New Jersey was. Some of the New Jersey links were possibly that Graham was sending money to Josephine who could have moved to New Jersey, or Rice may have recounted the wrong state. Graham also had a link to New Jersey ever since he hooked up with Nellie.

Joe Risley, her stepfather, was from New Jersey, and may have had relatives there. Is it possible that Graham was sending money to Nellie via Risley's family, rendering the money untraceable? Graham may have been still wanted in Utah, and would also explain the money being sent in unregistered letters by someone else, as it is suspicious that Graham just didn't mail any funds himself.[142]

In August, two months after the cabin shooting, the dying Graham was still alive, yet papers told how he was most likely going to die from his wounds but by mid-September he was well enough to eat in the dining area with other inmates. The Leavenworth Daily *Commercial* reported on October 30 that writers visited the Territorial Prison for Sunday Services, and Georgie was fine, looked penitent, and his fine, booming singing vice was loudly heard singing along to the hymns. The same article warns that Mr. Thornton, present at his recapture, had better watch his back.

In late November the Leavenworth *Times* showed it was keeping up with its former law-abiding citizen by warning that Graham was almost recovered from his wounds, and states that President Grant, favorable to Graham because of his military service, would likely pardon him if he would obtain the required recommendations. The article closes with Graham's promise to lead an honorable life if given a fair chance. The *Times* probably wondered along with everyone else at just how many fair chances had he blown.

The *Weekly Arizona Miner* wrote on New Year's Eve, 1874, that two men were arrested on suspicion of trying to assassinate Fowler by spying on his home at 758 Champa St in Denver. There was not a follow up.

In March, newspapers wrote that Graham was the only one in the prison who was required to wear iron jewelry constantly. Now he was a real Iron Clad Boy. As for the mining town of Rosita, the Canon City papers predicted "good times ahead for Rosita." For example, the Pocahontas Mine had paid its debts and owner Mr. Theodore W. Herr said the mine would be worked vigorously.

An article was printed in the *Chieftain* praising David Prosser, the latest warden of the Colorado Territorial Prison. According to them, Prosser dealt with the prisoners as if they were schoolchildren. The convicts were being kept busy doing construction. The new stonewall enclosure and lime kiln were products of prison work. It told about the large library for the convicts' use but does not detail any of the two hundred books. The Colorado *Daily Chieftain* gives us a rare look behind those bars and into Graham's life. The somewhat naive reporter took a trip to Canon City's prison and quickly found "Father" David Prosser. Prosser was attending to most of the convicts, who were working. The only prisoner not doing something constructive was "Maj. Graham."[143] He claimed illness again but was in fine enough condition to stand at his cell doors and stare at a window opposite, quietly contemplating the outside world. Graham is no longer the Ethan Allen of days past: the reporter tells us that Graham looks beaten down and compares him to an Alexandre Dumas character in the Bastille. Though the writer tells Graham that he advises the convict to learn his lesson, he believes Graham is indeed so broken and disgusted with it

all that he will probably not attempt another escape and will take the straight road upon release.[144] The *Chieftain's* hopes were in vain.

---

[142] Colorado *Daily Chieftain*, June 9, 1874
[143] Graham was referred to in papers by this time as Major Graham while ignoring the fact that he was a disgraced officer.

August 1875. In Washington DC President Grant was in the White House amidst growing scandals. George A. Armes was fighting to get his captain's rank back despite being humiliated by Secretary of War William W. Belknap who would have his own scandal. Public hearings were printed with signatures of officers who had only heard of Armes by word of mouth but were pressured to sign petitions claiming that Armes was everything from incompetent to illiterate. Benjamin Grierson was still with the 10th U.S. Cavalry. Call it a combination of Graham's Luck, networking, and old favoritism, when he walked out of the Colorado Territorial Prison on Aug 13, before his term was up, because of "good behavior." The *Chieftain* out of Pueblo followed the whole Graham saga from start to finish and asked on Sep 5 what many were thinking, and would have no clear answer to: did the definition of good behavior include overpowering a guard, breaking out of prison, and looting a town?

The actual records for Prisoner 75 included his conviction, notes about escape, his scars, and this: an Act of Congress released him. An act had been recently passed that allowed prisoners an early release based upon good behavior!

As for the other interesting items in those prison records, Graham told the Territorial Prison upon admittance that he was from New Bern. If he posed as a North Carolinian to maneuver a brevet from President Jackson, that was manipulation. Going on the record in a Colorado prison however as being a Southerner is peculiar.

Getting back to Canon City that autumn, David Prosser was requested to resign for unknown reasons.

Immediately upon his release on the 13th of August, Georgie went north to Denver on the evening train from Cañon City.

Inn early September it was reported that Graham was "sojourning" at Rosita, the town whose inhabitants he had robbed the year before. Why he chose to sojourn there is anyone's guess. Another told the reader that Georgie was looking at going to mine for Black Hills gold.[145] Somehow he went in the opposite direction. In any case he didn't stay long in Denver, perhaps he picked up his belongings or did try to get in on an expedition to the Black Hills.

Rosita was growing wonderful crops, mines were booming, buildings were being erected at a fast pace, and there were no less than three hotels. Tyndall Street was the main road, and many businesses stood on Tyndall including a jewelry shop and saddlers. It all would have grown considerably in just the short time Graham trekked through before. The post office was a gathering place in evenings when mail would arrive.[146] The town was growing with such rapidity that it was not out of the question to imagine the county seat being moved to Rosita. Back in June of 1874, the Canon City *Times* ran a paragraph on its front page from the citizens of Rosita, stating in part, "...They will defend Themselves against all who are Trying to Swindle them out of Their Mines. A Fair Warning to all Who Contemplate Rascality."

---

[144] Colorado *Daily Chieftain*, April 22, 1874.
[145] Las Animas Leader. August 27, 1875.
[146] The Letter Drop Inn restaurant now occupies the site of the post office.

It's hard to imagine how the citizens of Rosita tolerated the man who robbed them the year before, the same man the town had to hunt down, indeed the same angry escapee who'd vowed revenge on the men who found his hiding place. It wasn't long before he made himself a swaggering nuisance by wandering the saloons, causing trouble, and finding himself in the employ of two fast talking crooks, Col. J. R. Boyd and Walter Stewart.

The two men set up a bank with their eye on eventually stealing the money and skipping town. They took over the Pocahontas Mine whose vein of silver was discovered in spring of 1874 and owned by Mr. Theodore Herr of Denver who was out of town. Some of Herr's holders sold their claims to Boyd and Stewart, who began claiming the mine as their own. Graham and a new gang of about twenty-five ruffians then took over the mine, probably being paid by Boyd and Stewart who would later denied doing so. Local newspapers wrote that something was in the air, a feeling that it was about to get very dangerous.

Herr filed lawsuits regarding the mine. He attempted to continue work but found Boyd's hired thugs, led by Graham, occupying it, so he had to take it to the courts. On Sunday, Oct 10, Graham started agitating the men who had been working for Herr. The *Chieftain*[147] reported that Graham was provoking those men into violence.

It is assumed that Graham knew who was nearby. President Grant, whom he once stopped just short of claiming as a friend, and a man who wrote his endorsement for entry into the Frontier Army, later signing off on his court-martial, was in the Colorado Territory, getting as close as Colorado Springs. It would have meant nothing to Graham now.

James Pringle, who aided in Graham's capture from the prison escape, was now at the receiving end of threats from Graham who forgot about his promise to lead a straight life. He was also flexing his muscles at those in Rosita who aided in his capture. Summer was over, President Grant was on his way back to Washington, and the territory would soon be a state. Indeed there was change was in the air.

On the evening of Oct 11, 1875, Graham was in top form. He and a few pals[148] were openly drinking in the streets and waving their guns around and harassing people, as they had a habit of doing on most nights.[149] He then walked into a saloon and spotted James Pringle, one of the men who had participated in Graham's capture in 1874. At around midnight a fight ensued between a sloshed, revengeful Graham and the harmless Pringle who'd just left work. At least one gun was drawn and by the time Graham strutted back up Tyndall Road, Pringle was left with a shot in the foot.

Though the well-liked man wasn't killed, Graham had finally pushed an entire town past its limit. He had earlier "volunteered his service" to help in case there was to be

---

[147] Colorado Daily Chieftain. Oct 15, 1875.
[148] One was named by Boyd as being Mr. Lydon and Mr. Duke. An E. G. Duke from Kentucky did reside in Rosita and is buried in Silver Cliff Cemetery.
[149] Binckley and Hartwell, (Southern Colorado: Historical and Descriptive of Fremont and Custer Counties with Their Principal Towns. Cañon City, and Other Towns, Fremont County. Rosita, Silver Cliff, Ula, and Wet Mountain Valley, Custer County), 1879.

any trouble. Yet again Graham placed himself in a volatile situation to incite trouble, only to then selflessly offer his expertise in handling the situation.

He had just burned up his final "fair chance.

It was probably a quiet evening once Pringle's wound was attended to and when the men of Rosita gathered to talk. Graham was up at the Pocahontas Mine drinking with his comrades. The men of town may have debated on the details, for example, the Lynching Tree stood handy, on a ridge within view, but overall it was decided what to do. The good people of Rosita would take back their mine and rid themselves of a pain in the backside.

Graham's guardian angel was now the one on sojourn despite a warning. Sometime that night Boyd told Graham that shooting Pringle was a mistake and that he would be hung for sure. Graham was also told to leave, as Boyd and others were afraid he would get them all hanged. Graham, in a drunken stupor, claimed that Pringle shot at him first. Boyd later recounted that Pringle never pulled a gun on Graham, and that Graham slept off his drink in the ore house near the mine.

Daybreak, Tuesday Oct 12, 1875 began with a hung-over Graham making his way to town. Versions differ as to the exact details but the fact is Rosita hadn't slept, and it was waiting. According to contemporary reports[150], saloons and businesses were told to remain closed. Some say Graham saw the men, panicked, and tried to run away. One account said that he tried to run past the townspeople and attempted to take a man's gun.

Still others swore he clearly knew he was outnumbered and pled for his life, crying that he would flee to Mexico or elsewhere if let go. No matter the details, Major George Wallace Graham was shot to death then and there. The handsome grey-eyed New Yorker, whose name survives on a marker at Goldsboro Bridge, NC, and one of the original Buffalo Soldiers, was now riddled with at least twenty bullets to his athletic body.

On that same day the coroner's jury gave its findings.

> -- We, the jury summoned to hold an inquest over the dead body of Geo. W. Graham and to inquire into the cause of his death, do find that the same was caused by gun or pistol shots in the hands of a person or persons unknown to this jury. Signed James I. Gray, Geo. S. Barlow, F.R. Ford, E.S. Morgan, J. Labkin, R.P. Best –

The Denver *Daily Times* tells us the short tale of his funeral, such as it was.

> There is something ludicrous as well as sad in the funeral of the late Maj. Graham at Rosita. It would have been better for him had he died in the noble service of his country during the war than to have met such an inglorious fate.

His funeral is thus described:

> About 2 o'clock the funeral of Maj. Graham passed through the dense crowd that lined Tyndall street. In a small open wagon, drawn by a mule team, was a $5 coffin containing the body of Graham, and the driver sat on the coffin. Behind the wagon

---

[150] Ibid.

walked one solitary pedestrian, a constable, who felt that having a corpse on his hands, it was his official duty to bury it. And thus was put under ground all that remained of this wicked and desperate man.

It was rumored that his body lie in the streets for hours until it was tossed down an unused mine shaft, but the fact that there was an inquest and quickie funeral procession indicates that Graham is in an unmarked grave at the Rosita Cemetery. Another witness, George Kettle of Denver, was in Rosita at the right time to see Graham's $5 coffin being buried "in a gulch near town." Kettle also stated that even though he obviously didn't know Graham, he did hear "more than a thousand" versions of what happened.[151]

Since that inquest simply left the killers as unknown, we see that the town was close and covering for each other in that Western vigilante justice, for everyone would have known who was involved. This article also gives another interesting revelation if true. It claimed that after he had been shot outside that cabin upon his recapture, the men who found him sat around Graham in a sort of "Indian circle" with the intent to wait for him to die. Someone mentioned that they should just take him to town to die, which set in motion the wheels for another event in Rosita. It also calls his clemency from imprisonment after his court-martial a mistake.

Three days after his death, the *Daily Chieftain* squeezed in the following between "an amusing story" and another beginning with "the most enjoyable affair of the season."

> *--A gentleman from Rosita who was present at the capture of Maj. Graham states that Graham begged hard to be released, offering to go back to the penitentiary for life, or to leave the country immediately. He was told that he might run for his life, which he proceeded to do, attempting to grab a shot gun from one of the captors as he started. He was soon riddled with bullets. Our informant says that Graham was a bully and a coward, and took part in the mining difficulty from pure meanness, with the hope of obtaining an opportunity of shooting someone. His great aim seemed to be to rule the whole camp, but he finally died with his boots on, as most men of his stamp do. –*

The editor also made note of the irony that the only death in the whole affair was Graham's and that he was the main cause, and pointed out somewhat sarcastically that his death was no great loss, the town would survive well without him.

Josephine and Nellie would have heard the news as papers had a field day with Graham's third and final obituary. If Nellie talked herself into believing that he would return, she now knew it was never going to happen because, coincidentally or not, two weeks after Graham's death, Ellen "Nellie" Adams took a husband, George W. Mower.

The papers ran the incredible but not surprising bit that Graham almost survived yet again. It states that out of 36 balls to his body, only 4 were in vital areas.

He Is Finished

---

[151] Daily Rocky Mountain News, 15 October, 1875

Writers from the *Chieftain* arrived in Rosita the morning after his death. They were a bit surprised to find the town in a state of total normalcy, miners doing their jobs, restaurants busy, everyone notable in their ordinariness. Who knows what they expected. The gist was that the violence and Graham's battered and bloody body on the ground less than 24 hours earlier had never happened. The only oddity was a band of armed men on horseback called the "committee of safety" racing through the street on an errand of mercy, not trouble. This large committee, it came to light, was the same group Graham faced on his last walk into town. Recently formed, mainly because of Graham and his fellow ruffians, they claimed that Graham had been ordered by Boyd to shoot at anyone approaching the Pocahontas Mine. Graham actually boasted of doing so, but his combined egomaniacal lying and drunken stupors make his claim questionable.

Newspapers around the country ran the final obituary of "Major" Graham. Many had to educate people outside Colorado of the events, but it read like a dime novel. An oft repeated article in the days following his death read: "*The life and adventures of this man would, if correctly told, furnish material for dozens of such books as appear under the title of 'Jack Shephard,' 'The Forty Thieves,' 'Captain Kidd' etc.*" Or, the author may add, another man from England's Essex: Dyck Turpin, highwayman and horse thief.

Now, it was only after his death that one other bombshell was uncovered, concerning another woman. The citizens of Leavenworth must have known, but let the secret out after this obituary was finally recognized as being the one to stick: On the day that Graham was arrested for his impending court-martial in Kansas, he was preparing to be married to a prominent Leavenworth citizen's daughter. The marriage was to have taken place the day after he was arrested. Would he have stood up the young lady at the altar or was he preparing to commit polygamy? Josephine Graham was still his lawful wife. The Leavenworth fiancee's name is still unknown as no one ever made public record of it, but we can be sure it wasn't the sheriff's daughter.

Or was this, like so much of his life and death, another cooked up story to sell papers?

> A DESPERADO has died with his boots on. An account of his death will be found on another page. Graham was a man of nerve, possessed of the courage of a lion, but as unprincipled as his Satanic Majesty.

> **Another Loyalist Gone Home.**
>
> The hero of the subjoined sketch was for some time in command of a gang of loyal cavalry at Newbern in this State during the war, and by his marauding exploits kept all the old women, cripples, and their chicken coops, in the surrounding country, in a tremble of alarm. But he wore the loyal blue, and that made his cowardly assaults on unprotected farmers "daring enterprises" and his insolent abuse of noble Southern ladies—"unflinching patriotism." It is to be hoped he now enjoys his loyal society with Thad Stevens, Stanton, Sumner & Co. in the brimstone country.

The Denver *Daily Times* ran an erroneous summation of Graham's life on Oct 15, 1875. It went on reiterating the usual heroics including the Goldsboro Bridge firing and Graham posing as a Confederate that had arrested his own Union lieutenant, but the author (unnamed of course) claims that he first met Graham in North Carolina while Graham "was a sergeant in the Third New York cavalry." This anonymous source went on to say that Graham's promotion to lieutenant came from the Goldsboro battle. The *Times* writer could not possibly have seen Graham in the uniform of a Union sergeant, yet these errors (sometimes outright lies) would cloud future research and make us wonder how they even started, or if they were concocted by those already wishing to change Graham's past even after his death. Graham's own files state he entered the service as a 2nd Lieutenant.

It is astonishing that by the end of 1875 he was becoming a forgotten footnote. It would seem that the people of Rosita wanted to move on from Major Graham as quickly as possible.

He wouldn't give in to obscurity that easily. Another example of Graham's kismet? After lying in an unmarked grave for nearly forty years, his name was finally carved upon a tombstone. In eastern North Carolina, not far from his first fight at Young's Cross Roads, within mere miles as the horse gallops from Newport Barracks, Pvt. Norris (remember him from the North Carolina days?) lies buried. One of his wishes, carried out, was that his commander Capt. Geo W. Graham's name be placed on his stone. Evidently Norris felt something due to Graham. Despite having no marker on his exact burial spot, he is marked for eternity on someone else's. The owners graciously allowed me to photograph it and asked that it be noted here that it is on private property.

Mystery at a Museum (NARA)

On April 18, 1877, less than two years after Graham's death, George E. Spencer, Chairman of the Senate Committee on Military Affairs, sent a request to Army Adjutant General Townsend, wishing to view the recommendations giving Graham a commission in the 10th U.S. Cavalry. Spencer added that he wanted the copies as soon as possible. Yet the request was filled, with Spencer being sent copies "marked from A to J inclusive."[152] Those enclosures included Grant's recommendation, a few general orders dating from 1863 and 1864, and unnamed papers. I have been unable to find any reason why Spencer wanted to check records of a dead, cashiered officer unless it had something to do with Armes's fighting to get back his own commission. U.S. Grant's signature is on one recommendation. Was someone looking for evidence that President Grant had very questionable judgment? And how did Washington DC have those copies when Graham was given them back after his dismissal in 1870?

With so much of Graham's dealings it is interesting to note what is missing from records. Entire months of his service from company books. Medical records. NARA File 1854ACP1877 (the request from Spencer) seems to be incomplete.

Again in 1885, ten years after his death, those records were pulled again for no reason that I could track down. The Assistant Adjutant General, C. McKeever, received a request from the Treasury Department for dates of Graham's commissions in the 10th U.S. Cavalry and court-martial. The only surviving piece of this request is the reply. The information was duly given. At first I thought this was a relative's attempt to collect a pension, but the last line of the reply is odd enough that I ruled that out. It reads, "He had no leave of absence (*illegible*) to June 14, 1870." Someone in the treasury was asking if Graham had taken leave in 1870.[153]

I decided to examine Armes's court-martial from the spring of 1870 to see what Graham references there may be. Imagine my surprise when the folder only contained 4 scraps of notes, each in a clear protective sleeve. Every court-martial put upon Armes was literally missing. An old brown note, written by a clerk in December of 1887 states that a very diligent search was made to locate those files but turned up nothing. Obviously they have never re-appeared or they would be back in their place. A list of the generic charges and findings was in the folder along with a letter from Belknap himself stating that this particular item had signatures of 17 officers who did not want Armes to have his brevet rank restored, as well as letters from pro-Armes officers. Those have vanished also. My thoughts are that Belknap and possibly Grierson destroyed all of the court-martial files, and then claimed that since nothing existed to base it on, he would be denied his brevet. It is also possible that, as outspoken as Armes was against Belknap and his sutler scandal, something incriminating may have been in those transcripts. There are literally no records at NARA regarding Armes's courts-martial.

---

[152] George W. Graham's Military File. National Archives, Washington DC.
[153] File 3852 ACP 1885, National Archives, Washington DC.

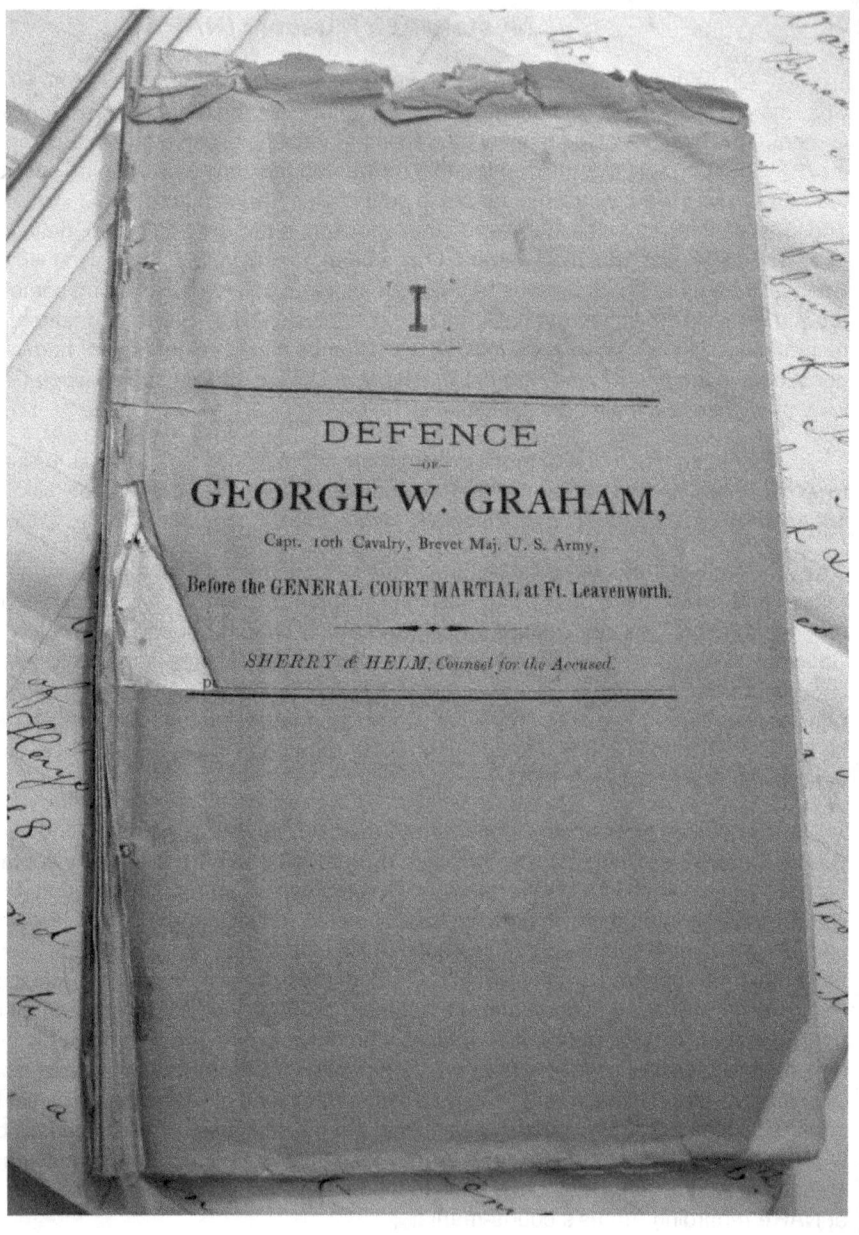

(Graham's Defense, words, style, grammar and punctuation, in its entirety)

Mr. President and Gentlemen composing the Court Martial[154]

In opening the defense in this case, which had occupied your situation for so long a period, and has been conducted with such vindictive zeal, permit me to return my sincere thanks to each and every member of the Court for the uniform courtesy extended to me on all occasions, and the unflagging patience and attention accorded me in producing the testimony of witnesses scattered over a large extent of territory, the nature of whose evidence it was impossible, in many instances, to know until examined on the stand, and some of the most important of whom I have been unable to procure. For many months previous to this trial the energy of enemies had been devoted to the preparation of a case against me, and much time was necessarily consumed in the effort to refute their accusations, and to meet by counter proof the various charges preferred. And yet, with all their expert handling, when arraigned before you it seems that out of fourteen specifications originally preferred, eight of them were abandoned for reasons easily divined when you recall the spirit in which the prosecution was conducted. Malice overreached itself and only evinced its disposition to wrong me by the preference of charges which it was impotent to establish. The elegant and accomplished Major Armes, to whose regard for the public service I am indebted for my appearance here, was not present to confront me, but the Judge Advocate has perhaps exercised as much skill in restraining him from mounting the witness stand with his black book, as he has in confining others of his trusty witnesses in the guard house for the acknowledged fear that their sturdy Spartain virtue might be tampered with.

The charges are, First ---- Conduct unbecoming an officer and gentleman. The first specification under this is, in substance, that I rode through the camp of the detachment of the 10th Cavalry, near Ft. Hays, about the middle of May, A.D. 1868, with a notorious prostitute in my buggy by the name of Annie King.

Although my Post Commander, Major Yard, did not seem the alleged offense worthy of notice, yet the Proux-Chevalier Armes, felt scandalized at the exhibition, and hence a year and half subsequently preferred the charge. I can only regret my inability to procure the attendance of Annie King to testify upon this point, feeling assured that her evidence would be promptly admitted by the Judge Advocate, inasmuch as he produced the same character of evidence in prosecuting the aforesaid Major Armes, and stoutly contended that a woman could testify truly, and that her evidence was competent, although she was a Cyprian. But I have been unable to bring her forward as she is without the jurisdiction of the Court.

The witnesses for the prosecution are Lieut. Davis, Col. Carpenter, Lieut. Banzhaf and Lieut Myers. The majority of these gentlemen doubtless were honest in their impression that the woman with whom I was driving, about the middle of May, A.D. 1868in the afternoon, was Annie King. None of them were near enough to know positively, and none at that time had ever spoken to her, except Banzhaf, who had known her some

---

[154] The names Mrs. Moses and Mrs. Kuykendall have been found in a few census records but nothing of value as to their relationship to Graham.

years before, he says. He also says she gave him some token of recognition, not so emphatic as a bow, however, and passed on. Nobody saw this but Banzhaf, and Mrs. Moses was not known to the other officers. There is no question but that the impression prevailed that the occupant of the seat in my buggy on that occasion was Annie King. But in a group of idle men when one makes such a remark as, "there goes Graham with Annie King in his buggy," it takes very little observation on the part of the loungers to come to the same conclusion.

Is it very probable that I, with half a dozen sworn enemies in camp, would openly drive before them in the glare of sunshine, to give them an opportunity to assail me? Were I accused of some reckless act of drunkenness—some disgraceful act committed in a moment of passion, there might be some plausibility in this idea; but for a man whose home has always been on the outside of a lunatic asylum, it seems a very unlikely story. The want of reason in the matter compels strict proof of such extraordinary conduct, and we have the *opinions* of some excellent gentlemen as to the identity of the woman. The evidence shows clearly that they were mistaken, or as the Judge Advocate would say, when attempting to lay down some peculiarly illegal proposition, they were "palpably and manifestly" wrong in their impressions.

But what say the witnesses for the defense? Mr. H. C. Fisher says he knew Annie King very well; that about the middle of May (the same time also) he saw me driving with a lady in my buggy between Fort hays and the Camp. This lady was not Annie King, and he knew her not to be. He knew it because he was compelled to exert himself to get out of the way of the grey horses I was driving at the time, and took that *good* look at the people in the buggy which persons generally take when compelled sharply to stand aside from pursuing wheels. He knew her *not* to be Annie King, whom he did know very well. He remembers no veil, which she had probably raised as she was on the road and not driving through camp at the time, but in the direction thereof.

Sergeant Burke also testifies that at the same time of day and about the middle of May, he saw me driving towards the camp, where the witnesses for the prosecution saw me, and that I was accompanied in my buggy by Mrs. "Mosby," as he calls her, but Mrs. *Moses*, as he evidently means. He knew the lady – knew it was her, and had time and opportunity to examine, because, he testifies, *I stopped and got him to hitch my check rain*. He *knows it was Mrs. Moses*, and had taken such a chance to see that he could not have been mistaken.

Sergeant Augustus, of my troop, was next called, who substantiated the evidence of Serg't Burke, and added that he had seen me riding with Mrs. Moses and Mrs. Kuykendall several times.

Another witness testified that Mrs. Moses was in appearance not unlike Annie King, which may account for the mistake made by the officers who testified for the prosecution.

Mr. Joyce is very positive that on the same occasion the woman with me was not Annie King, but Mrs. Moses. He knew them both, and I knew that I was riding with Mrs. Moses. He knew also, as is testified to by other witnesses, whose testimony the court will recall, that the impression in camp was that the woman was Annie King. He knew the mistake, and proposed for himself a complicated series of wagers, which none but the most erudite sport could either understand or appreciate, and which had no more to do with this case than it had with the International Alabama Claim imbroglio. Nobody but Justice Joyce would have made such bets, but Joyce would have perished before he would have bet any other way.

Now here are four witnesses who swear positively that the woman with me on that occasion was not Annie King – all but one say it *was* Mrs. Moses, and one testifies to a similarity on their persons. It is also shown, by at least two unimpeached witnesses, that this must have been the same occasion, for the reason that the same excitement was raised in camp on that day about my driving through camp with the supposed Annie King, and it is not proved by the prosecution that I ever drove with her through the camp but once. This, then, must have been the occasion as the time and all the circumstances correspond.

The Court is doubtless, aware that I am entitled to the benefit of any doubt that may arise as to my guilt. Is there a member of this Court who can say, after recalling to their minds the evidence under this charge, that this woman with whom I was riding was unquestionably Annie King? Will they accept the impressions of comparative strangers, rather than the convictions of those who knew the woman as well as the lady with whom I was actually driving? The presumption is that there is no desire on the part of the Court that I should be convicted, and it is impossible for me to conceive how men of intelligence, not actuated by prejudice, or blinded by previously formed opinion, could hesitate upon this charge. All I ask is that the *evidence* shall be the guide and measure of the Court's decision.

As to the relations which the Judge Adv. attempted to establish between myself and Annie King, I have but little to say. These relations are pretty well shown by Malcolm Graham, one of the witnesses for the prosecution, who was found un bed with her – said he never found any difficulty in sleeping with her for the money, nor heard of any one else, so fortunate as to have the greenbacks, being sent away "onsatisfied." Still this had nothing to do whatever with the charges preferred against me, and I am perfectly aware that the record was loaded by the Judge Advocate with that purely irrelevant matter simply with the view of wounding the feelings of an officer whose hands were tied and whose onprotected and helpless condition should have protected him from insult. How did it affect the charge of my riding with a prostitute, that she should be my kept mistress? "Palpably and manifestly," in no way whatever, and evidence on that point was impertinent and gratuitous.

The second specification under the first charge is that I attempted to sell a horse to Lieutenant Maxon. This was the roan horse, and the answer to this specification will be contained in the reply to the other charges, in which the same animal is the subject of the charge. Lieut. Maxon proves an offer on the part of myself to sell him the horse early in October, A.D. 1869. If the horse was my own, or if I reasonably supposed him to be my own, the offer to sell him could in now wise be considered criminal. He says, however, that he would not have purchased the horse under any circumstances, as he understood that Maj. Armes "supposed or claimed" *that the horse was a Government horse, and was anxious for some one to buy him, so that he could get grounds to prefer charges against Major Graham.* It will be seen then that at that time Armes was lying in wait, and that it was a notorious fact that he was on the look out for grounds upon which to have me arraigned. And yet I am charged with openly and publicly taking a public horse, which my notorious enemy supposed to be a Government horse, and trying to sell him. This does not look very natural and should require very strong proof to establish.

But let us examine all the testimony upon the question as to the manner in which the horse came into my possession.

Lieut. Banzhaf is the first witness examined after Lieut. Maxon, on this point. The question is put to him: "State when you first saw the horse (the roan horse), and where;" and the answer is, "In October, 1868, at Fort Wallace. *A trooper was riding the horse from water to the stable."* He then goes on to state that he remarked to Lieut. Orleman and Col. Carpenter that he admired the horse and would like to buy him. He then asked one of the men how long he had been in the company, who told him that he joined the day before and was one of the last from Leavenworth or Hays. Questioned by the accused, he replied to the time when he first saw this horse, that he was being ridden by a trooper. He repeats this in another place. He also testified that the horse had "an odd sore on his nethers, an old fistula."

After some time had elapsed Lieut. Banzhaf was recalled when the following questions and answers were propounded to and answered by him.

Q. Do you remember a detachment of horses brought to Fort Wallace for the troop of the accused, in October, 1868?

A. Yes, sir.

Q. How were they brought there?

A. A detachment of "I" troop, 10th Cavalry, was sent to Sheridan for them.

Q. *Did you see those horses coming into Fort Wallace?"*

A. *Yes, sir.*

Q. State if you saw among them the Roan Horse which has been called the Amick horse?

A. Yes, sir.

Q. In what part of the detachment was he?

A. I don't remember: he was led by one of the men.

Q. When did you next see him?

A. As I have stated, when I saw a trooper riding him to the stable.

Again he is questioned.

Q. Do you remember whether he was branded or not?

A. I did not see any brand at that time. I saw the brand when I saw the trooper bringing him up for water.

Q. When was that?

A. *A few days after the horse came in.*

Now compare this statement with his original testimony. He first says that he saw the horse being rode by a man from water to the stable. In his subsequent statement he says he first saw the horse being led with the detachment that came from Hays or Leavenworth. In his second statement he states that the *next time* he saw him he was being rode by a trooper.

Now in his first statement he distinctly says that he asked a trooper how long this horse had been in the Company, and that the trooper told him that the horse came in. He states in his second testimony that the second time he saw the horse that is when the trooper was riding him when he was being brought into Wallace with the detachment.

Q. When did you next see him?

A. As I have stated, when I saw a trooper riding him to the stable.

Q. Was it the same day or the next?

A. *The same day.*

Comment is unnecessary on such discrepancy. The most ingenious mind can contrive no excuse for such previous false swearing on a point most essential in the case. His further description of the horse as to his sore back is contradicted by every witness, both for the prosecution and defence, who testified as to the appearance and condition of the horse. If Banzhaf's testimony were uncontradicted I cannot see how it could be relied on, but it is flatly contradicted, not only by himself but by others.

Private Gallatin Smith testifies that this roan horse was in the Company's stable when he first saw him, before being issued. When he was issued, Smith says he was a little lame, and in such bad plight that none of the troop desired him. Banzhaf said he was sorebacked and had the fistula. Smith says he was lame and in bad condition. Both say he was branded.

Private Peter Johnson, whose character was impeached by private Lane, one of the rebutters, says he remembers the horse as being one that came with a detachment from Sheridan, and that Lieutenant Amick got him. Johnson don't remember much, as he says he was just then on the eve of another term in the guard house, where he vegetated for the next three or four months.

Private Isaac Evans is called for the prosecution, and reveals the startling fact that this horse was once in the Company Stable, but how or when he got there he knows not. Lieut. Amick afterwards had him. This gentleman don't even remember that any horses were drawn that year. He only remembers that they drew horses once at Fort Wallace, but whether he saw it before or after he does not know.

Private Gibson said he saw the horses with the men all the way to Wallace. In order to give him Banzhaf's statement we would think that he arrived just before reaching Wallace, and led him in.

The Judge Advocate before bringing in this swarm of things, testifies that he sent for the men who were of the detachment that went to Wallace after the horses at the time referred to, that from what Gallatin Smith told him, and what he saw himself, (of the nature and details of which he does not see fit to inform the Court,) he thought they were being tampered with. He therefore put them in the lock-up so that their virtue might be retained intact and their effectiveness as witnesses unimpaired.

It is not a little singular that whilst the Judge Advocate sent for Jones, Underhill, Gibson, Sanders, and Lane, to Col. Nelson, as being of the party who were sent to Sheridan for the horses, he should in the first place have neglected to have subpoenaed Sergeant Brown, who commanded the detachment? It turns out that Sergeant Brown and Private Hopkins would be very indifferent witnesses for the prosecution, and they were not subpoenaed, although one was the commander of the party and the other present. The Judge Advocate says: "I learned then on inquiry who the men were who were of the party who brought the roan horse from the cars at Sheridan to Ft. Wallace, and sent the names of them to Col. Nelson by Major Kidd, with the request that if the information proved correct, and they had been of that party, to send them up her," &c. The charges had been carefully prepared and witnesses subpoenaed by the dozen, yet Sergeant Brown, the most important witness for the prosecution, if he would testify favorably, is omitted. Perhaps Gallatin Smith knew and guarded as such the Judge Advocate had the privilege in which their very person was unknown to all make them and were produced at a time when it was impossible to get full proof of the detestable character they have in the Company.

Reexamination shows that these men were private soldiers and all swore enemies of the non-commissioned officers who have testified here for the defense. There was not one of them who had not been put in the guard house time and again by me, and, as the evidence discloses, had been chronic grumblers about their rations and other rights, to the infinite annoyance and disgust of myself, Lieut. Amick, and the other officers, both commissioned and non-commissioned, of the troop. Yet these men, I suppose for the promotion of good order and discipline, are brought here to impeach the evidence of the men whose superior qualifications and character have made them worthy of being put over them. The Court must exercise some discretion as to the respective statements of conflicting witnesses, and decide according to the preponderance of evidence. With this principle in view I have not the slightest fear as to the conclusion to be arrived at by unbiased minds.

I have honestly endeavored to give the substance of all the evidence produced by the prosecution with references to the manner in which I came into possession of the roan horse; I shall now proceed to relate the prominent features of the evidence for the defence as applicable to the same point.

It is pretty well established than in and about October, 1868, at least two detachments of horses were distributed among "I" troop. There were several roan horses among them. Sergt. Brown certainly brought a detachment from Sheridan somewhere about the time I became possessed of the roan. But Sergt. Brown says he was at the stable when this roan horse was brought in; that Bombray brought him in and said that I had won him in a race. He goes on to state that it was *not* one of the horses which he got in the detachment in Sheridan, and that he would have known if it was. He states the time and says that Lieutenant Amick came in from a scout just about the time the horse was brought in by Bombray.

Now here is the man who drew the horses among which the roan is said to have come, and the only responsible man in the detachment, and he says he not only knows the horse was not among the lot turned over to him, but was present at the time the horse was brought to the stable by Bombray, who said I won him at the race, and knows that horse to be the Amick horse I am charged with having taken from the Government. Brown is not impeached, and there can be but one reason for not believing him, and that is that he has testified for the defence. He certainly had the best opportunity of judging.

Serg't Charles Junior remembers very distinctly that the roan horse was brought to the stable tied behind my buggy and that one of the boys remarked that the Major had got another horse. He says he would have known it if this horse had been issued by the government, and that it was not. He remembers that this occurred immediately after the Sand Creek fight, which somebody told him was in October, whereupon the Judge Advocate entered into a very lengthy cross-examination as to the time of the Sand Creek fight, which possibly may have occurred a few weeks previous to the time Junior heard it had. In the Malcolm Graham charge a difference of a dozen or so months makes no odds, but it is a splendid triumph of genius upon a most material point to wring from a colored Sergeant, after two hours badgering, the fact that he might have been mistaken two or three weeks.

Private Hopkins was one of the detachment that went with Serg't Brown for the horses at Sheridan. He says this roan horse was not among the number then drawn and given to Brown, (who never got but one detachment from Sheridan,) and that Gibson drew another roan horse there, which he has had ever since. Gibson said he rode the Amick horse. Some colored "pusson" has been committing an impropriety! Perhaps it may be Hopkins so he has not been submitted to the moralizing influence of Col. Merrill's patent virtue preserver vulgarly known as the guard house, but skeptics may be disposed to doubt whether the free air of Heaven may not have as beneficial an effect upon human integrity as the more confined atmosphere of a post prison.

Sergt. George Augustus remembers distinctly when the horse came, was standing at the stable door when the buggy was driven up with the roan horse behind it. He knew it was not a Government horse, and Bombray told him then and there that it was won that day by me in a race. This was the 1st Sergeant of the troop.

But happily for me there were those present on the occasion when the horse same into my possession whose testimony is direct and unmistakable. Mr. Goodale was present by invitation when the race took place, and Sergt. Bombray rode my horse, "Stocking-legs,: which won the race from a Mexican.

Mr. Goodale testifies that he was invited by me to attend and did attend; that he saw the race, and that I won; that the horse was the roan, known as the Amick horse, and that I took him home with me, tied behind my buggy, Bombray riding "Stocking-legs." He was quite sure at the time he first testified that Lieut. Amick was present, but upon reflection immediately went to my counsel, Gen. Sherry, and told him of his mistake as to Amick being there. Gen. Sherry advised him at once to see the Court or Judge Advocate and mention the circumstance stating his desire to change that portion of his evidence. Mr. Goodale further testifies that he did go to the Judge Advocate and express this desire, when he was abruptly treated by Col. Merrill, who told him he could attend to it on Monday.

His statement is borne out by that of Gen. Sherry, who saw him go up to Col. Merrill as if to speak to him, but his back being turned he could not see whether he spoke or not. Col. Merrill testifies flatly that he did not open his mouth to him on the subject. There is a conflict between the Judge Advocate and Mr. G. which only the attendant circumstances can decide. The Judge Advocate was certainly very intensely occupied with the case in which he felt.so deep an interest, and it may b that he paid attention to what was going on. Picture, however the absurdity of the condition of things his testimony would portray. A man goes to counsel and tells him that he desires to change his evidence. Counsel refers him to the Judge Advocate. The man desiring to make the change walks up to the Judge Advocate and stares into his countenance without saying a word. There is no necessity for this – no reason why he should not have spoken to him—he had just been advised to do so by a gentleman on whose judgment he relied, and yet he goes up to Col. Merrill and gazes into his face without saying a word. Why should not Goodale have told Col. Merrill? He had mentioned his mistake to Gen. Sherry and afterwards appeared to correct it. Would it not be a very bold and exceedingly silly man who would tell such a gratuitous and pointless falsehood, and one so readily susceptible of detection? Which is it most difficult.to believe—that Col. Merrill with his mind fully engrossed by the case in its progress, should abstractedly give an answer which he does not remember, or that Mr. Goodale should perjure himself upon a point where there is no earthly necessity for so doing in order to accomplish just nothing whatever? He could have changed his testimony as others have done without a word with the Judge Advocate, and yet he prefers to make of himself both a fool and a liar for the special benefit of the prosecution!

It is a most unpardonable sin for a witness for the defense to change his evidence, when reflection shows him he has made a mistake; yet how unclouded and serene is the brow of the Judge Advocate when Major Kidd, a witness of the prosecution, changes and makes a little more stringent *his* testimony. "The case being altered, alters the case." Mr. Goodale afterwards saw the horse when in Lieut. Amick's possession, and recognized him as the same horse.

Private Arthur Bombray is examined; says he was at the race – rode Stocking-legs and won the roan horse from the Mexicans. He is as consistent in his dates as could be expected of one with his few advantages, and his testimony is unshaken by the prosecution. The roan horse he knows was won on that occasion, and that he was the identical horse owned afterwards by Lieut.

Amick. He brought him home with me and describes all the details of the race. The Mexicans had lost one horse that he could see, and that was this – yet upon close examination, he chose to remember seeing some horses grazing at a considerable distance off. Suppose they had had no other horse, would it be anything remarkable for a Mexican in a country where horses were so abundant to bet his last horse? The only wonder is that he didn't lose his carryall and shirt.

Bombray's evidence is positive and in order to disregard it, he must be found guilty of the grossest perjury.

Lieut. Amick testifies that about the middle of October, 1868, he was at the stable where I kept my horses and that he saw and admired this roan horse, that I told him he might see him, and afterwards gave him the horse on condition that if he was sold I should have one half the proceeds of the sale. He also testifies that it was a day or so after I got the horse that he saw the horse, and that I told him I had won him in a race with some Mexicans. He was busy at that time making up my papers, and says he would have known if I received the horse from the Government, and that I did not. He further testifies that this was not at the time of Serg't Brown's bringing a detachment of horses from Sheridan, whilst Brown testified, it will be remembered, that he only brought one lot from Sheridan. The horse was not branded, that he could then see, and he did not discover it until the following May when he shed his hair.

Lieut. Amick also testifies as to the statement given to him to Major Kidd for Col. Nelson concerning the title to the horse. Major Kidd says that he approached him and requested some evidence of his title to this roan horse – that Amick told him I had a Quartermaster's receipt for it, and that he would see about it. This Lieut. Amick denies positively. He says too that Lieut. Amick give him a statement substantially embodying Major Graham's account previously given of the manner in which he obtained the horse, and that he returned it on account of its not having the date inserted when the said horse was won from the Mexicans. That Amick gave him the required amended statement, and that he gave it to Col. Nelson – that Col. N. put it away, lost it from his portfolio with other papers, and afterwards found what he, Col. Nelson, considered the identical statement, furnished by Amick, with the other lost papers. Major Kidd says he looked at the recently found papers and discovered a difference chiefly in the word and date, which he, Kidd, had outlined in the first papers furnished. That Col. Nelson said that it was exactly the same paper that had been furnished him. Now, Lieut. Amick denies furnishing but one paper, and says that the statement read here in Court is the same and only one furnished Col. N. Col. Nelson is a very particular man, as has been proved here — had had his attention particularly called to this statement, and especially the question of date, and it does seem that he would be able to identify the document which he had demanded and examined, as well as Major Kidd, who procured it for him. Lieut. Amick testifies that when Col. Nelson missed the paper he immediately called on him for a copy, which he furnished forthwith, and which Col. Nelson accepted. This copy is almost identical with the one found in the portfolio after its supposed loss. *Col. Nelson* thought it was the same paper given him – his attention had been called to the defect in what Kidd calls the first statement – he had instituted the investigation and still thought the paper he found the one furnished him by

Amick. Nor did he more than acquiesce in Kidd's views of the case. He simply *took Kidd's word against his own opinion*, and that is all Kidd testifies to. You are called upon then to disregard both the opinion of Col. Nelson and Lieut. Amick, in order to believe Major Kidd. The question then arises as to what point or object there could be in my having taken that statement from Col. Nelson's private portfolio or of Amick's having taken it from the same place. If the date *had* been furnished Kidd as he says it had, did we not know that fact, and did we not know that it could be proved by both Col. Nelson *and* Kidd? Has any contest or dispute been raised as to the date by me, or has the trial disclosed any reason why the date should be an important matter? I am, and always have been, willing to acknowledge that it was about the time Kidd says the "missing" document mentioned as the date of my obtaining the horse, that it did come into my possession. If I wanted to steal the paper I certainly would not have taken others also, and after taking them what would have been the necessity by substituting others without the date? Would it not have been taking a chance of detection to accomplish nothing whatsoever?

You are called upon then to disregard the opinions of Lieut. Amick and Col. Nelson, and believe Maj. Kidd in order to come to the conclusion that I stole a paper which could so no good, and the like of which on the part of the possession could not possibly benefit me. Can the Court disregard the opinions of Col. Nelson and the positive evidence of Lieut. Amick, and believe the opinion of one that I perpetrated as most silly, pointless, and unnecessary theft?

As to the brand on this horse, there is such contrariety of opinion that it must remain a subject of doubt in the minds of the Court. Lieut. Amick says no brand could be distinguished at first on the horse, and is supported by several witnesses, whilst Banzhaf says he saw it distinctly, and several others say the same thing. The question, however, is not whether the horse was branded, but whether I came into possession of him as a Government horse.

The first specification under the second charge of "wrongfully and knowingly selling or disposing of Government property," is that I sold or disposed of a Government horse to Capt. Badger.

Capt. Badger testifies that I never sold or gave him a horse, but that I simply loaned him a horse to ride to a trip, and designated the place where the horse was to be left. There is no charge that I sold or disposed of the horse to Capt. Byrne, so that I am not called upon to meet that charge. Capt. Badger didn't know whether it was a Government horse or not, but I have no hesitation in saying that it was.

Captain Badger also states a fact which it is very important to observe, and that is, that I did not trade him the horse for a bull dog. He failed to state, however, whether the bull dog he gave me was branded, or whether he was a Government dog at all.

The second specification is, that I sold the inimitable Banzhaf a chestnut sorrel horse, the property of the United States, sometime in August, 1868. Banzhaf says that the horse was branded – a chestnut sorrel, and described by me as a horse belonging to Lieut. Mullins. He says he was under the impression that it was the horse of an officer in the 5th Infantry, Lieut. Mullins. In the intervals of his examination (brief, he was generally on the stand whilst here) he made a statement to counsel to the effect that he knew the horse was not the Mullins horse, but that he testified as he did to make it easy on me; that he knew it was a Government horse and belonged to a trooper in "I" troop, as counsel thinks.

If Lieut. Banzhaf made this statement, unquestionably he cannot be believed. He denies having made it, and it remains for the Court to decide as to the amount of credit he is entitled to. My counsel at once told the Judge Advocate of the circumstance, who informed the Court, and action was immediately taken, so that he had an opportunity of explaining, which he did by denying any such remarks on his part. The Court must judge as to the truth or falsity of his explanation.

Lieut. Mullins proves that I sold no horse for him – that he sold one to Lieut Pepoon, and that I kept one some few days and gave it back to him, which horse he afterwards disposed of.

But Sergt. Burke and Corporal Smith chanced to have me purchase this horse – one says on or about the first of May, and the other about the first of April. The latter statement was made by Corporal Smith, the Company farrier, who says he might be mistaken as to the date; at any rate the difference is immaterial. They both saw me buy him a few months before, and both know he was the horse I sold to Lieut. Banzhaf on or about the first of the following August.

Mr. Goodale also remembers that I purchased a sorrel horse about that time, received a bill of sale, which he subscribed to as a witness, and that I paid the owner in his presence for the horse. All the efforts of the Judge Advocate to shake and weaken his testimony were unavailing. In this cross-examination of Goodale, the Judge Advocate became facetious. He wanted to know if the man who signed the bill of sale *looked* like a person who could spell well; also if he *looked* like a man who could write a good hand. He, with equal propriety, might have asked him if he appeared as though his grandmother was named Eliza Jane and his wife's uncle a skillful hand at paring his toe-nails.

But all the witnesses remember seeing me try the horse, and state the circumstances of my riding up and down the streets. He was not branded then apparently, but if a brand came out afterwards, it was no evidence whatever that he was a Government horse – only that he once had been. As Burke testifies he certainly never was turned over to me by the Government.

The third specification under this charge refers to my disposition of the roan horse to Lieut. Amick, and has been sufficiently discussed.

The fourth specification is that I sold or disposed of a Government horse to Col. Crosby.

Col. Crosby testifies that he received as a loan from me a horse which he returned, and that it was a Government horse. As I am charged with selling or disposing unlawfully of the horse to Col. Crosby, it would seem that when he proved the horse was not disposed of or sold to him at all, no further evidence should have been allowed. But the Judge Advocate proceeds to examine him, and the Colonel states that from what I said he inferred that I could sell the horse to him, and advised him to buy it. As I stated no price, and did not make a formal offer of sale, of course this is no legal attempt to sell. But if I did urge the Colonel to buy the horse, and his inference, if such he made, was a most violent one. I had the right, as was the custom, to loan horses to Gen. Sheridan's staff, as I did in this case, and if I had desired to sell the horse, as a private horse, I would scarcely have gone to a member of Division Head Quarter's Staff. The fact is, that I may have recommended Col. Crosby to purchase the horse, but he would have been compelled to have bought him from the Quartermaster, which I knew he could do; or I might have bought him and sold it to him. The letter written by Col. Crosby to me, complaining of my having attempted to get him into trouble by selling him a Government horse, resulted from a misconception on the part of the Colonel, which must be apparent to all.

But what has this to do with *selling* him a horse? I am not charged with attempting to sell him a horse, and the horse had been returned by him.

A most unjust and unjustifiable departure from the proper sphere of the prosecution was the attempt to prove by Lieut. Pepoon that the horse was afterwards owned by Col. Stone. Was it not proved by Col. Crosby, as well as several others, that the horse he borrowed was returned to me? And is there any charge have preferred that I ever sold a horse or disposed of one to Col. Stone? Is this thrown into the record as innuendo or why is it that the Judge Advocate inserted in the evidence what he knows that Col. Stone was present a few weeks ago, and that he examined him with reference to what he knew concerning my having sold horses to him, and that he knew nothing whatever. I complain then most bitterly of this illegal proceeding and feel confident that the Court will sustain me by rejecting its consideration altogether.

The last charge against me is of having created a disgraceful row in a house of ill-fame with Malcolm Graham.

The objection as to the discrepancy between the time alleged in the charge and the time proved having been overruled, it only remains to say what must have been apparent to the Court, that a personal difficulty with a man, resulting from insult.to me at an hour when none were present, save the actors in the difficulty, is scarcely entitled to the appellation of "disgraceful disturbance." Would it not have been more disgraceful to the uniform I wear to have suffered myself to have been called "no gentleman," in the rough terms of Western vernacular, than to have promptly resented it? That certainly was my interpretation of it. I went into the house because I deemed it my duty so to do, and the fact that admission was refused made me suspicious and determined me to go. Lieut. Pepoon may construe general orders differently from myself, but I certainly esteemed it my duty to visit that house at the time and in the manner I did, nor did I conceive that because I was in uniform I was compelled to listen to the coarse insults of Malcolm Graham. He himself testifies that there was no disturbance raised to attract attention from any person, and Sergt. Augustus distinctly swears that, although at the front door when I went in, and remaining there until I came out, he heard no noise. I reported the affair next morning as officer of the day to Major Yard, Commander of the Post, who thought it perfectly proper that the affair had died out, and of my memory, until the meek and Armes felt outraged on behalf of the United States Army, and preferred the charge.

    In conclusion, permit me to remind the Court that these charges, preferred by Major Armes, is response to Charges previously preferred by me— in fact within ten days after the preferring of mine against him.

    I have endeavored to state and comment upon the evidence to a spirit of candor and truth. I now my own innocence of every charge preferred against me, and confidently leave my case to the careful consideration of those whose duty it has become to sit in judgment upon me.

GEORGE W. GRAHAM

Capt. 10th Cav. And Brvt. Maj. U.S.A.

Epilogue: The Other Players

Col. Joseph M. McChesney resigned in May of 1865 and died that autumn from wounds received earlier that year when he approached the Confederate lines by ship without the flag of truce being raised. The Associated Press reported in September 1865 that a monument was "being planned in his memory."

Josephine Graham was finally identified after publication of the first edition. She seems to have lived somewhere in New York until George's death, when she went to Colorado with their son. It is my feeling that she wanted to have her husband reinterred but failed. In 1885 she is listed as having some sore of paralysis in the Colorado census. Josie lived in the Witter Block of Denver until her death from consumption in January 1888. She is buried in Denver's historic Riverside Cemetery.

In March of 1889 **George A. Armes** wound up in trouble for allegedly pulling the nose of Pennsylvania Governor James Beaver, repeating his habit of nose tweaking. Apparently, Armes was originally on the list of those selected to ride in the Inauguration Procession of President Harrison. A few of Armes's old enemies saw to it that his name was removed. Armes showed up anyway in full dress uniform on horseback and rode anyway. When he later confronted Beaver, he demanded an apology from the governor. Beaver refused, Armes allegedly tried or succeeded in pulling Beaver's nose while Beaver pushed away Armes hand. Armes was tried for the offense, even after sending a formal, written apology to Beaver. Armes stated that he would prefer suicide to a court-martial, stating that if that happened, Beaver would be guilty of murder. Meanwhile, some 100 citizens of Pittsburgh ordered an engraved medal to be presented to Armes in gratitude. The item was described as gold, with a bar and pendant shield. It was inscribed, "Presented to Major George Armes by 100 subscribers in approval of his pulling Gov. Beaver's nose." It was sent to Armes with a letter from the fundraisers telling that they represented most of Pittsburgh, and calling Beaver their "alleged Governor."

He was married and divorced several times, made a killing in real estate in DC, as well as parts of Virginia, including owning some of what is now Appomattox National Battlefield. Armes never stopped hating Graham and would claim all his life that officers of the Tenth and the US Army in general were torturing him for proffering those charges on George. As late as the 1880s, as Armes fought to get his rank restored, he would refer to himself as a "young officer."

For a fascinating, self-aggrandizing read on George A. Armes, see his autobiography, *Ups and Downs of an Army Officer*. But take it with a hit of salt. Other sources show that Armes was capable of having the language of a so-called sailor, but not in his auto bio!

Anna Barr, aka **Annie King**, was listed on her marriage records as being born Anna Johnson from Texas. She married Captain William Barr on Oct 5, 1872, with the 2nd MO Cavalry's chaplain uniting them. Witnesses were well-known Missouri attorney Lucien Eaton and Anna's sister Celia Pierson. She was granted a pension in 1866, after William died from chronic diarrhea related to disease. She turns up again after the Graham incidents in May 1874, filing for Barr's pension. Apparently, by moving to Kansas and

Colorado she assumed the monthly pension would accrue, but without her picking it up, she was dropped from the pension list. She, with the assistance of Eaton and her sister, now going by Celia Groves, had to reapply for that pension. Her reasons given were that she was unaware that by not collecting it she would be dropped, and also that she "did not need it" when she was living in Carson City, C.T. $20 must have been unimportant to a woman who never turned down a greenback. Letters to her lawyer tell how she bought her own house back after she sold the contents, inventory showed her love of pineapple, brandied peaches, and bourbon. King wrote to her sister from Denver in January of 1871, complaining that it had been a bad year (was she referring to Graham's cashiering?) and in 1874 she applied for Barr's pension again. Barr married a miner named Mark Bidell and moved with him to Colorado, who had been a merchant in Leavenworth about the same tie as she and Graham had lived there. In Colorado they owned several mines including Crystal Hill and lived in Bonanza, across the Sangre Christo Mountains and Custer County where Graham died. The Biedells had several children and Annie died Oct 26, 1908 of stomach cancer. The woman "who never sent away a man unsatisfied" knocked ten years off of her age on later census records, and apparently hid her baudy past by becoming active in the new Catholic Church in Del Norte. Annie also listed her place of birth as Spain on one census, Old Mexico on another, and Texas on still another. She gave her parents' birthplaces as ranging from Spain to Scotland! She has no gravesite, as she was cremated at Riverside Cemetery, ironically where Josie Graham lies.

The 10th Cavalry at Ft Sill ordered a court-martial against 1st Lt. **Silas Pepoon**, accused of cheating at cards. Though Pepoon begged that the probably false charges be dropped, he was denied. In 1874 he used his gun to commit suicide some eight miles away from camp. He had recently suffered malaria and was noted as suffering from melancholia. In the ensuing investigation and scandal it was deemed the location of the 10th was partially to blame for everyone's actions leading up to his suicide. The 10th Cavalry was relocated to Texas, in part because of this.

Two weeks after Graham's death, **Ellen Nellie Adams** finally married a George, George Mower to be exact. He was 16 years her senior. Mower was in mining, and his sister Sarah married a wealthy man, Isaac Requa. Nellie would have two more daughters, Lucy Shaw Mower and Sadie Requa Mower, named after wealthy sisters of their father. Both girls by Mower were left sizeable inheritances by their aunt, including an apartment building, the Brown Apartments in Salt Lake City. Notably, Belle was left out of the wills, probably treated like the "bastard child." "Utah Nellie" died in February 1926. It is unknown what she told Belle about Graham.

Belle Mower had been purposely left out of the wills that gifted her half-sisters with wealth. What she knew about her father is unknown, but she certainly was aware that her stepfather's family looked down upon her. She was married in 1889 to Samuel Reggel, born in England to a Russian immigrant, and who tried mining in the early 1880s but decided that running gambling dens turned a quicker profit. He turned his mansion into part home and part roulette/faro joint for wealthy out-of-towners. At least one marriage took place at their home on 255 West Fifth South, the groom a dispatcher of the Rio Grande Western, the bride a friend of Belle's. The friend, Minnie Nugent, was the widow of a man shot in a gambling house. Belle and Sam split in 1900 while she was involved with a married man, John H. Benbrook, and the two of them went to Nome to find their fortunes in gold while she was still married to Sam. At this time, the friend of Belle's who was married in her home was involved in her own mini-scandal. John Benbrook's brother

Smithy, also a married man, tried to divorce HIS wife and run off with Minnie. Belle spoke to the Salt Lake *Herald* at the end of 1900, using the name Mrs. Reggel. Belle must have inherited something from her father: Benbrook, a hustler, owned a gambling den with his brother Smithy, the Sheep Ranch, in Salt Lake City. In 1899 John Benbrook shot and killed a man over a woman (neither Belle nor his wife) he'd been dining with. Benbrook's wife filed for divorce, charging that he'd left her and their baby son with no support while he ran off with girlfriend Belle Mower to Alaska. They were wed Feb 12, 1901, two weeks after his divorce was final. When their marriage was announced in the local paper, Samuel Reggel complained that Belle used the name "Belle Reggel," and he wanted it known that they were absolutely divorced and disliked her using his name, indicating the hate between the two. Benbrook was later questioned regarding an automobile that ran down a former Army officer, Col. James Jackson. The car had at one time been registered in his name. The Benbrooks moved to Oregon, where John died seven months after Nellie Adams's death. Belle died in 1960. She had no children. One of the only samples of her quotes is the following regarding turn of the century Nome, Alaska: "I think Nome has a great future before it. The first rush in there was too great and of course many people were disappointed. Some prospectors expected to scoop nuggets up in the shovels, but when they found they couldn't do that they came away and the said the country wasn't any good. There is plenty of gold there, but the people have to work for it, just the same as anywhere else." At this time she was in Nome with a married man, using the name of the man she was married to and cheating on. Belle may have been denied a material inheritance but she certainly inherited her father's traits whether she knew it or not. Benbrook died in the 1920s but Belle lived until 1960, leaving no children. Any belongings are sill undiscovered.

George Witherell was arrested again for murder in 1888. As he was being taken to jail a posse was formed. Storming the jail late at night they tied up the guard, not to hurt the officer but just to do their job with freedom. Witherell was dragged away and strung up on a telephone pole in Canon City, CO. The lynch mob proudly posed for a photo. The photo of Witherell hanging from a line has been used in many television shows on hangings as filler, but never identified. Grisly souvenir hunters took Witherell's suspenders and various other items, and one person even ripped off his moustache, taking part of Witherell's upper lip with it. These pieces were all framed in one "collection," later sold at auction. The buyer's name was private and never located. The Royal Gorge Museum rightly feels that the display, no matter how ghoulish, belongs to the citizens of Canon City and should be at the Museum.

J. R. Boyd was incredibly lucky that he survived with his neck intact. He was given his freedom under the condition that he would pay off money he owed and get the hell out of the territory. He did so, returning to the Topeka and Kansas City areas where he had lived earlier. It was said that the six-foot, heavily built man was a former Confederate Partisan Ranger, or Bushwacker, and retained the moniker "Colonel" for the rest of his life. He had previously been Mayor of Baxter Springs, KS and shot the sheriff there before coming to Colorado. In a quirk of coincidence, one of the witnesses was Dr. Bradbury, later of Rosita, and whom Graham robbed. After Rosita, Boyd was almost hanged but bribed a guard with his gold watch. He made it to Canon City. Boyd wound up not only a free man after a stint in the Penitentiary, but the Topeka *Daily Commonwealth* called him a "gentleman…interested in mining affairs" when making notice of his marriage in 1878 to a well-heeled Topeka girl. Boyd would later claim that Stuart, the "damndest thief he ever saw," also took him in. Choice words from Boyd, who, in 1884, was jailed for not paying a fine set upon him and others involved in the Idaho Prospecting and Mining Company, a sham.

Walter Stuart, whose real name was Walter C. Sheridan, blamed the Rosita occurrence on Herr, yelling that the latter had Stuart's guards arrested. Stuart also claimed to have had nothing to do with Graham, claiming Graham was just a saloonkeeper. It was found that the respected Stuart was actually a forger, faking checks on the Bank of England. Stuart would make his way to Canon City on foot, then New York. He was later arrested in Montreal for stealing a coat and died in prison.

Many of the **men involved** with Graham and the mine occupation fled to Canon City.

I have not been able to locate copies of the Denver *Mirror* from the time of Graham's death, so **Stanley G. Fowler's** opinion on Graham's death is unknown. The *Mirror* folded in the 1870s and Fowler moved back East.

After the *Mirror*'s demise he showed up in Virginia, early 1890s, as editor of the S.A.L. Magundi, a newsletter for the Seaboard Air Line Railroad Company, which operated on the Eastern seaboard. After his retirement he relocated to Los Angeles where he died in 1907 in what the papers called a "charitable institution."

James Pringle continued to be a town favorite after Graham was killed. His property was rumored to have been on the ridge behind the post office and the Lynching Tree. He is buried in Rosita Cemetery, a stone's throw from the unmarked graves where his nemesis may lie.

Several of **Graham's siblings**, as well as his mother, are interred at Forest Dale Cemetery in Essex County, NY. I was able to track down a few distant descendants but letters have been unanswered.

So, what do you think? Scoundrel? Civil War officer not much different than any other? Victim of his own recklessness or others' jealousies? Maybe like any of our own lives, the truth is some of everything.

I hope you've enjoyed reading this story as much as I've enjoyed and obsessed over writing it. I truly did my best. I am no professional writer but I hope the story makes up for my lack of skill in that area.

I am optimistic that this isn't really the end. I have more papers and items that weren't added, side notes and such. But there may be photos of the people in this book in an attic, knowledge of the NCUV flags, Josie's belongings… I would love to hear about them. Maybe that artillery sword at The History Place belonged to him. Maybe his grave will turn up. The key that was made and used in a prison escape? The Colt taken from a Confederate? A walking stick, perhaps broken in two? Flowery letters written to one woman or another?

For now I must say goodnight to you, Georgie. The ball is in your court, if you want to make contact, just knock over a book or lead me to another find. After all, I'm one woman you couldn't run from!

Fayetteville, NC. April 2018

Capt Graham With his men Returned from Washington N.C.

That is finished

Photo said to show original officers of Co. B, 24th NY Ind Battery. Graham was a member of the original five. If this photo is indeed of the Original 5, note the man seated at left bearing a strong resemblance to Graham.

Photo from "Civil War Brockport" by William Andrews

Sabers donated by a descendant of one of Graham's cavalry soldiers who idolized Graham so much he had Graham's name put on his gravestone. The bottom is a rare example of a saber used by the NCUV, and the top is an 1840 artillery sword with scabbard. Is it possible that Graham gave the soldier his sword?

FNW345CB1867

Adjutant General's Office,
Washington, D. C.
July 10th, 1867.

Sir:

I have the honor to acknowledge the receipt of your letter of the _____ day of _____, 186_, requesting a "Statement of Service" of _____. The following information has been obtained from the files of this Office, and is respectfully furnished in reply to your inquiry:

It appears from the Rolls on file in this Office, that George H. Graham was enrolled on the 15th day of Oct, 1861, at Crown Point, N.Y., in Co. Say 24 Regiment of N.Y. Battery (Rocket Batt.) Volunteers, to serve 3 years, or during the war, and mustered into service as a 1st Lieuten the 1st day of December 1861 at _____, in Co. __ 24" N.Y. Battery (Rocket Batt.) afterwards 1st N.Y.A. Volunteers, to serve 3 years, or during the war. On the Muster Roll of Co. ___ of that Battery for the months of Nov and Dec, 1862, he is reported a 2nd Lieut "Transferred to 3rd N.Y. Cav by order Maj Genl J.G. Foster Dec 24/62."

Muster roll of Co. "E" 3d N.Y. Cav for May & June 63 reports him a 2d Lieut "Transferred to 1st N.C. Cav May 1st 63." He was promoted to Capt & mustered in as such Oct 19/63 in Co. Z, 1st N.C. Cav ... as such until June 27/65 — which time he was mustered out of service.

Very respectfully
Your obedient servant

To _____
Assistant Adjutant General.
(6)

Graham's handwritten submission to the US Army for acceptance.

> P | 1 N.C.
>
> Bird Patrick
>
> Pvt., 1st Lieut. Graham's Cav. Co., 1 Reg't N.C. Vols.†
>
> Age 19 years.
>
> Appears on
>
> **Company Muster-in Roll**
>
> of the organization named above. Roll dated
>
> Plymouth N C June 20, 1863.
>
> Muster-in to date June 20, 1863.
>
> Joined for duty and enrolled:
>
> When Mch 30, 1863.
>
> Where Plymouth N C
>
> Period 3 yr months.
>
> Bounty paid $ 100 ; due $ 100
>
> Valuation of horse, $ 100
>
> Valuation of horse equipments, $ 100
>
> Remarks: ....
>
> *This organization subsequently became Cav. Co. L, 1 Reg't N. C. Infantry.
>
> Book mark: ....
>
> Meding
>
> (356) Copyist

Rare example of Graham listing his company as "Graham's Cavalry Company."

The Buffalo War Song.
(BY A NORTH CAROLINIAN.)

Arise comrades,—up! the camp fires are bright,
Come gather around their embers to-night,
For day shall return, but not with the scene,
Which twilight hath left with the sunset serene.

Our brothers now sleep in the dull silent grave,
Their blood shed by traitors appeals to the brave.
Our muskets are bright and ready for strife,
Revenge be the cry for each innocent life.

We know ev'ry forest and path and ravine,
We fear not their bloodhounds, our scent is as keen.
And long before dawn a dozen or more,
Shall land on the dusky Plutonian shore.

We'll give them a lesson they'll not soon forget,
Dodge and run as they may, we'll be up with them yet:
We'll teach them that outlaws, the black flag who raise,
Shall find, in due time, a sad end to their days.

Full well do we know that our cause is aright;
On the dear native soil of our father's we fight,
To defend the Republic is all that we ask,
And freely we each give our lives to the task.

The swamp's gloomy ambush, where Marion fought,
Was the scene where the feasts of a hero were wrought,
And wild as the haunts where the cypresses stand,
Shall be the war-whoop of the Buffalo band.

Beaufort, N. C., February 29, 1864.

Songwriter's name unknown but "Plutonian Shores" reference to Edgar Allan Poe illustrates Poe's popularity at this time.

Col Joseph M. McChesney   Brigadier Genera Innis N. Palmer

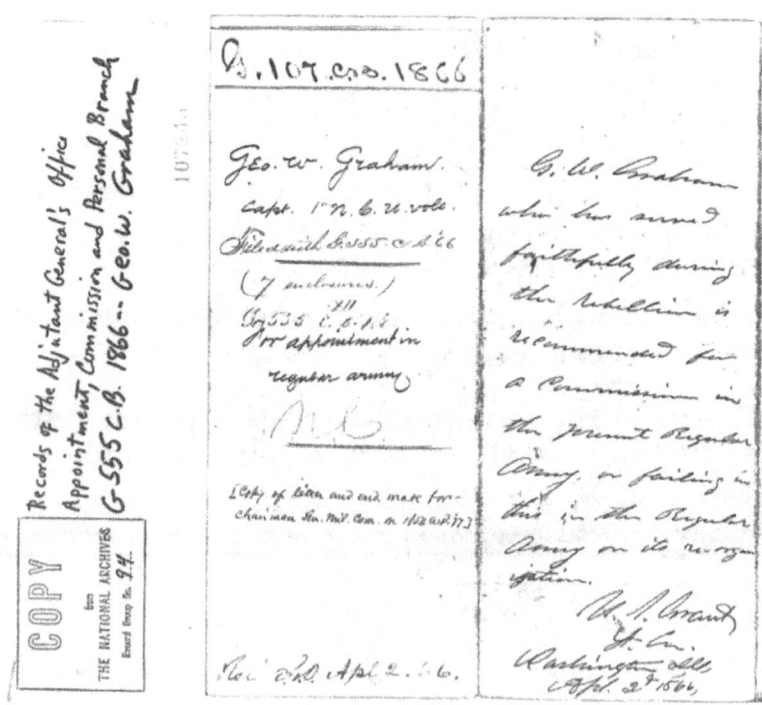

General U.S. Grant's recommendation for Graham to get a commission in the Regular Army after the war.

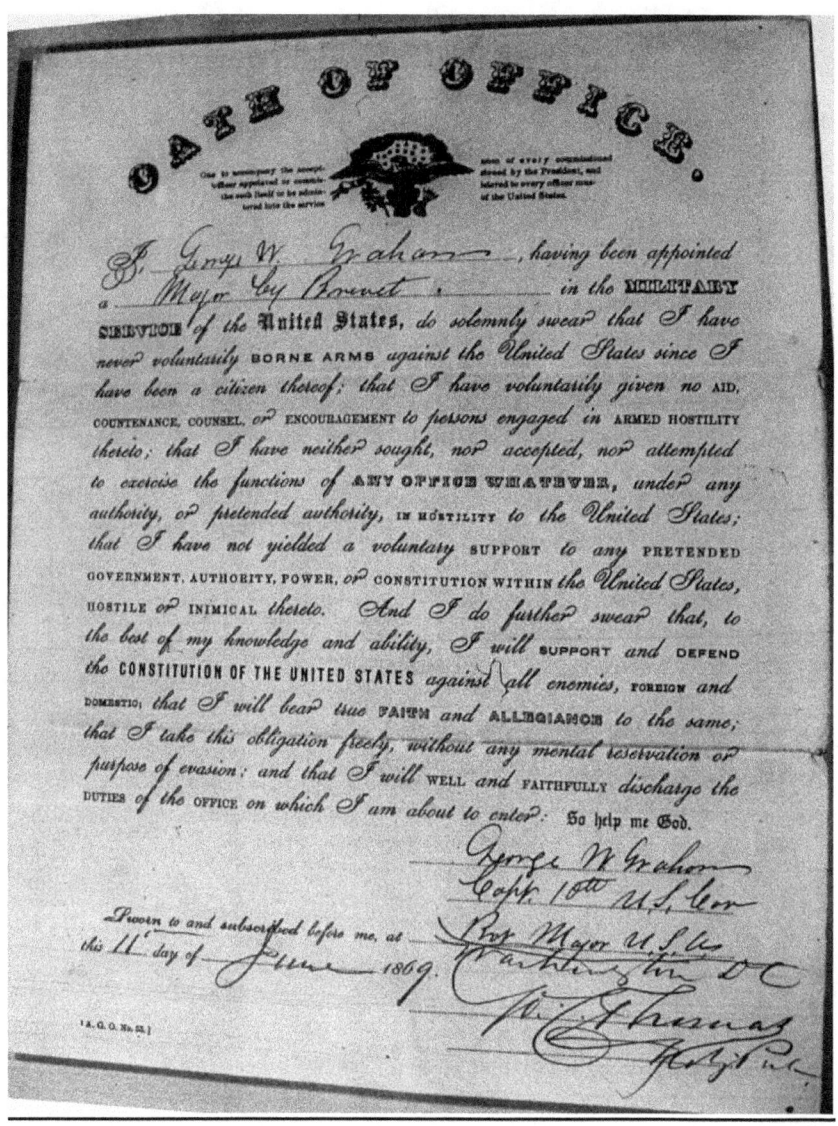

Graham's Oath as a Brevet Major signed in Washington, DC. By the end of the year he would be in arrest due to charges filed by a fellow officer. *National Archives*

After Graham returned from Washington, DC with his new brevet he stopped off at Leavenworth and had a photo made of himself. Note the insignia on his cap is a sewn on, embroidered patch.
Author Collection

Company F commander Capt. George Augustus Armes, (who must have set a record for being arrested himself), proffered charges against Graham, leading to the latter's court-martial.

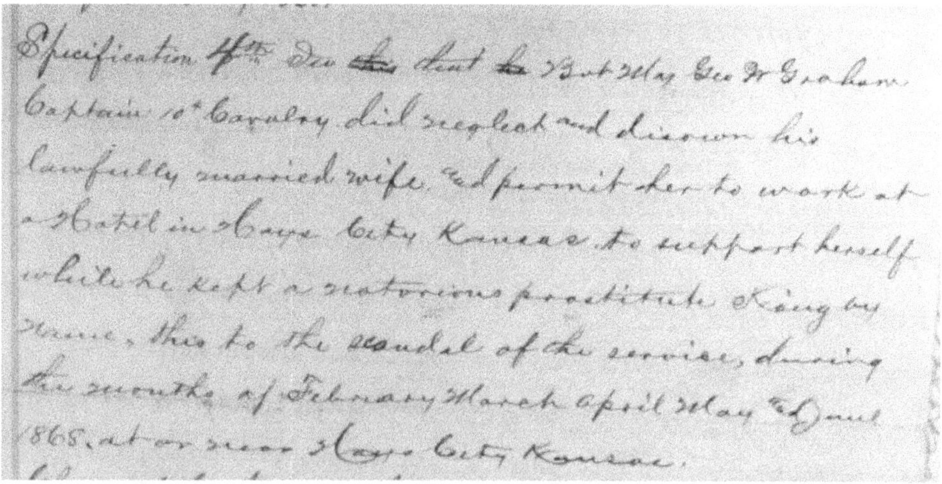

Specification 4th In this that Bvt Maj Geo W Graham Captain 10th Cavalry did neglect and disown his lawfully married wife, and permit her to work at a Hotel in Hays City Kansas, to support herself while he kept a notorious prostitute King by name, this to the scandal of the service, during the months of February March April May and June 1868, at or near Hays City Kansas.

One of the original charges against Graham at the start of his court-martial was abandoning Josie to keep a prostitute. However, this is the only place this charge appears as for some mysterious reason as the charge was dropped and not mentioned again in the proceedings. It was obvious from Annie King's letters to her lawyer that she knew Josie.

National Archives *Court Martial Case Files, 12/1800 - 10/1894. PP 1227. Record Group 153.*

and how much did it amount to, write soon and tell me all the particulars

Yours Respectfully
Annie Barr

Address
Annie Barr
Care of Mrs G. W. Graham
Hays City
Kans.

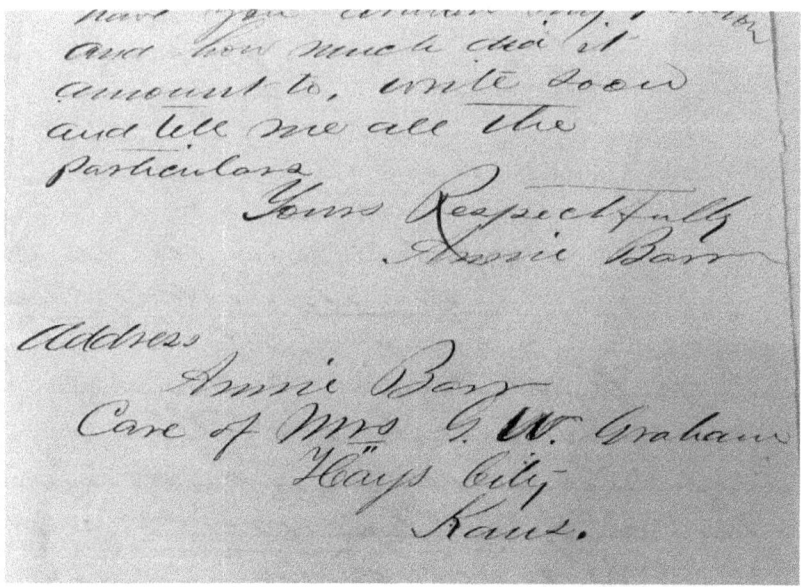

A most unusual letter. If we are to believe the accusations, Graham's kept prostitute was sending letters to her lawyer and instructing him to write to her in care of Graham's wife.

The Missouri Historical Society Archives

Warrant for Graham on charges of conspiracy to rob and murder paymaster Brooks, 1873.

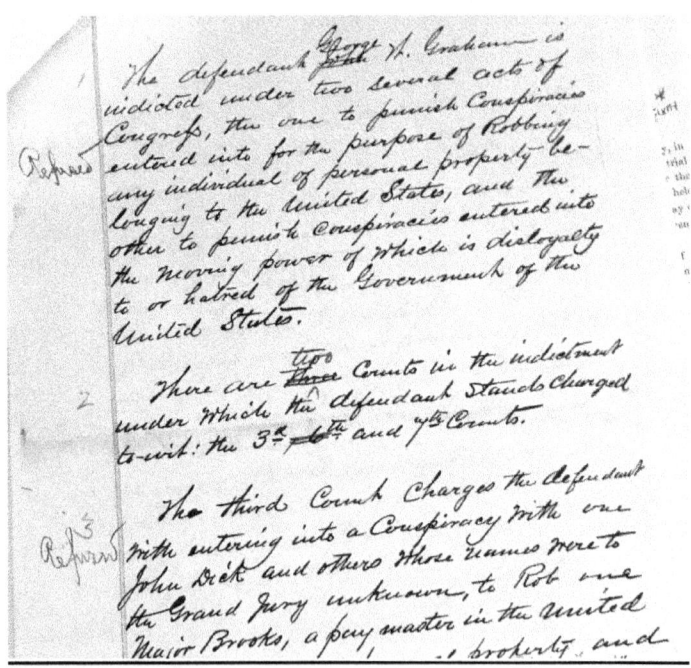

Graham and his lawyers had objections to what almost amounted as a kangaroo court. Every single one of his requests was marked "refused" as these papers show. *Courtesy Denver Archives*

Colorado Territorial District Attorney Hiram C. Alleman

Part of Graham's prison record. He gave his home as Newbern, NC. *Courtesy Colorado State Archives*

James Pringle on his property in Rosita, CO. Pringle was shot in the foot by a drunken Graham Oct 11, 1875, prompting the town to take the law into their own hands. *Courtesy of The Letter Drop Inn, Rosita.*

Denver businessman George Kettle was a witness to Graham's burial.

Graham's daughter Belle Adams Mower Reggel Benbrook lived until 1960. She died childless. Newspaper illustration accompanied story about her (future) second husband's murder trial in Salt Lake City, 1900.

Illustration from the Salt Lake Tribune

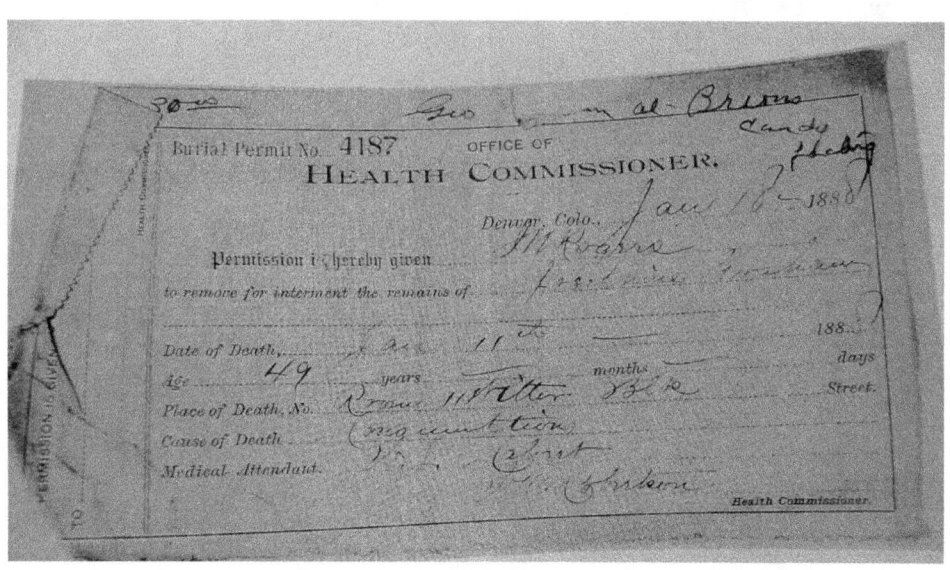

Josephine Jones Graham's burial permit, 1888. She lies in Denver's Riverside Cemetery. Top of form lists George Jr. and his employer as Brion's Candy Company.

Denver Archives

Josie Graham's resting place in Denver with my framed CDV of her husband.

Author Photo

www.ingramcontent.com/pod-product-compliance
Lightning Source LLC
Chambersburg PA
CBHW071703040426
42446CB00011B/1891